JULES LAFORG

Les Complaintes

edited by
MICHAEL COLLIE

UNIVERSITY OF LONDON
THE ATHLONE PRESS
1977

Published by
THE ATHLONE PRESS
UNIVERSITY OF LONDON
at 4 Gower Street, London WC1

Distributed by
Tiptree Book Services Ltd
Tiptree, Essex

U.S.A. and Canada
Humanities Press Inc
New Jersey

0 485 14713 0 *cloth*
0 485 12713 x *paperback*

Printed in Great Britain by
The Garden City Press Limited
Letchworth, Hertfordshire
SG6 1JS

Athlone French Poets

General Editor EILEEN LE BRETON

Reader in French Language and Literature,
Bedford College, University of London

This series is designed to provide students and general readers both with Monographs on important nineteenth- and twentieth-century French poets and Critical Editions of one or more representative works by these poets.

The Monographs aim at presenting the essential biographical facts while placing the poet in his social and intellectual context. They contain a detailed analysis of his poetical works and, where appropriate, a brief account of his other writings. His literary reputation is examined and his contribution to the development of French poetry is assessed, as is also his impact on other literatures. A selection of critical views and a bibliography are appended.

The critical Editions contain a substantial introduction aimed at presenting each work against its historical background as well as studying it genre, structure, themes, style, etc. and highlighting its relevance for today. The text normally given is the complete text of the original edition. It is followed by full commentaries on the poems and annotation of the text, including variant readings when these are of real significance.

E. Le B.

PREFACE

This edition of Jules Laforgue's first book of poems, *Les Complaintes*, is the first outside France. Two good French editions are in print: Claude Pichois' *Les Complaintes. L'Imitation de Notre-Dame la Lune. Derniers Vers*, Armand Colin (1959) and Pascal Pia's *Poésies complètes*, Livre de Poche (1970). Both editors corrected typographical and grammatical errors in the only available text, which is that of the first edition. The copy-text of the Athlone Press edition is the British Museum copy of the first edition published by Léon Vanier in 1885 to which the silent correction of obvious typographical and grammatical errors has been made in accordance with the policy of the Series. Not one of the corrections made could in the slightest way affect the sense.

I have made free use of J. L. Debauve's *Laforgue en son Temps*, Nizet (1970), the book in which he published for the first time part of Laforgue's correspondence with his publisher, Léon Vanier, and listed, also for the first time, the more significant differences between the first edition text and the sets of proof sheets that had come into his possession. It is a pleasure to have this chance to acknowledge, across the Atlantic, M. Debauve's invaluable contributions to the study of Laforgue. I also thank David Arkell for help with points of detail, my wife for a scrupulous proof-reading of the text, and Margaret Bowman for her help with the typescript.

A grant from the Minor Research Fund of the Faculty of Arts at York University, which permitted a vital visit to Paris in 1974, is acknowledged with warm appreciation.

M. C.

ABBREVIATIONS

RB	*La Revue Blanche* (available as Slatkine Reprint, Geneva, 1971)
V	*La Vogue* (Slatkine, Geneva, 1971)
EPL	*Entretiens Politiques et Littéraires* (Slatkine, Geneva, 1971)
GBA	*La Gazette des Beaux-Arts*
RI	*La Revue Indépendante* (Slatkine, Geneva, 1971)
C	*Les Complaintes*, Vanier, 1885
DV	*Derniers Vers*
LA	*Lettres à un Ami 1880–1886*, Mercure de France, 1941
ML	*Les Moralités légendaires*, Mercure de France, 1954 (first published 1894)
MP	*Mélanges posthumes*, Mercure de France, 1902 (i.e. Vol. iv of *Œuvres Complètes de Jules Laforgue*, Mercure de France, 1902–3)
QC	*Œuvres complètes de Jules Laforgue*, Mercure de France, 1920–30
SV	*Stéphane Vassiliew*, Geneva, 1946
PG	Debauve, J. L., *Les Pages de 'la Guêpe'*
Pia	*Poésies complètes*, Le Livre de Poche, Gallimard, 1970

CONTENTS

INTRODUCTION

Late in November 1881, the young poet, Jules Laforgue, travelled by train from Paris to Coblenz to join the household of the Empress Augusta of Germany, to whom he had been appointed as French reader. For the next five years he had to make himself available twice a day to read to her both from French and Belgian newspapers and from books and reviews she might find interesting.

It was his second job. Previously he had worked as secretary to Charles Ephrussi, art connoisseur and collector, helping him with the preparation of a book about Dürer's drawings. Still only twenty-one, Laforgue had lived in Paris for about five years, had failed to pass the *baccalauréat*, had little choice of career in consequence, and was in effect being rescued by the friends who recommended him for this position in Germany. As he travelled through the night, his first publication, *Les Complaintes*, still four years away, he must have been extremely relieved to be leaving behind the loneliness of his student days when, like so many others, he had lived at subsistence level in a single room on the left bank. Yet he must also have had mixed feelings about leaving France. A French writer was leaving Paris. Worse, he was going to Germany, not a place renowned in 1881 for its love of literature and art. Worse still, he was joining the Imperial German court, or a part of it, and would be as isolated from contemporary life as if he had been put in prison.

His first impressions were of the ancient coach that met him at the station, the dark façade of the palace, the sentries, the servants, and his set of rooms where, late at night, he was brought his first German meal. A Nihilist poet had slipped away from his garret in rue Monsieur-le-Prince and was now installed in the comfort of a German palace, where he had his supper in front of a cheerful log fire and fell asleep beneath a blue eiderdown.

His luggage contained only a few personal possessions, a small number of books including the poems of Baudelaire and Cros, as well as volumes by Taine, Balzac, Huysmans, Stendhal and

Hartmann, and several bundles of papers: the notes on Paris galleries which he had made while working for Ephrussi in the hope that, like Ephrussi, he might become an art critic; his notes on the books and lectures of Taine, whom he had heard at the Ecole des Beaux-Arts where his brother was a student; probably an unfinished novel; and almost certainly those early poems he had read to Paul Bourget and which he intended for a volume to be called *Le Sanglot de la Terre*. These were his secret. The Empress did not know she had employed a poet who, instead of settling to an orthodox life, had spent the last two or three years with café intellectuals, talking poetry, and assembling, analysing, re-assembling the anarchies of disbelief from passages in Hartmann, Darwin, Ribot and Schopenhauer. She saw simply a well-built, rather elegant, well-spoken, discreetly witty young man who was known to be informed about contemporary French culture. Since she rarely spoke German except when with her husband, for fifteen minutes each morning and evening, and since she had the good sense to be uninterested in German literature and art, Laforgue was what she wanted. Laforgue for his part did not reveal that his aim in life was to be a poet, not at least when he talked with ancient retainers like the Countess Perponcher, the Grand Mistress of the Household, or the Countess Hacke, Lady in Waiting (in perpetuity), or Augusta's secretary, M. de Knesebeck. These people cared nothing for poetry and Laforgue was not so foolish as to trouble them with what they could not understand.

In this way, one of the most brilliant French poets of the 1880s went briefly to ground. The decade was to see the publication of important books by Verlaine, Corbière and Rimbaud, the pro-liferation of little magazines devoted to *avant-garde* literature and art, the battles over Naturalism and particularly over the works of Zola, both his novels and his journalism, and the step-by-step acceptance of Impressionism, which meant in effect the liber-ation of French art from the 'Academy'. This was the period in which that perennial tendency of the artist to avoid the orthodox and to resist the rules of taste by which society limited his imaginative freedom was given new momentum in specifically, avowedly, anti-bourgeois, anti-religious, anti-social works, which at once constituted a critique of society and an opportunity for artistic originality. Eventually, in fact not long after Laforgue's death in 1887, the anarchy was seen to be 'literary' and tame; protest became respectable; and openly acknowledged scepticism reduced the need for hypocrisy in moral and religious matters. But when Laforgue travelled to Germany, just ten years after the Franco-Prussian War, novelists, painters, and poets were excited by an art which challenged established values, disrupted the social order and abandoned the coherence of logical and orderly discourse. Laforgue was part of this movement. As strongly as any of his contemporaries, he felt the need to reject the forms and principles of traditional art, particularly the traditional procedures for imitating classical art, and to replace it with something more appropriate to the times, an art which was ironic, sceptical, ephemeral, new. He spent his first few years in Germany thinking about how to achieve this and the result was the privately-printed, limited edition published in 1885 and called *Les Complaintes*.

In all likelihood some, perhaps most, of the things Laforgue did during 1882 and 1883 went unrecorded. The evidence of his letters, as we inherit them in Volumes iv and v of the second Mercure de France edition and in *Lettres à un Ami*, is clearly incomplete and may in some respects be unreliable as well; hand-tailored for the recipient as they had to be they avoided the genuinely personal. He may have written, in fact undoubtedly did write, quite a lot which never saw the light of day, including several attempts at a novel. On the other hand, there is no uncertainty about what most concerned him during those years. He had, very simply, two desires. The first was to make a book of poems. The second was to establish himself as an art critic. It was the inter-relationship of these two interests that led him to *Les Complaintes* and the route he followed obliged him to abandon his early poems and severely modify his ideas about art. Remarkably, as the Empress's household made its seasonal moves between Berlin, Coblenz and Baden-Baden, Laforgue came to terms with his own poetic predicament in the course of less than two years. When he arrived in Germany he had a naïve notion of what a poem was; by the spring of 1883, when he began to write *Les Complaintes* or, rather, when he began to see the 'Complaintes' he had written as part of a volume, he had invented an entirely new kind of poem which was consistent with his more mature attitude to art in general. Many poets develop in this way, but few have been as directly influenced by painting as Laforgue.

Except in some of the poems he wrote at school, Laforgue was not the type of poet who wrote directly about his own experience. Poems were not reports of actual events, nor was their main purpose the recollection of places and people. Poems consisted of words and the words were not used descriptively. Even in the poems which Laforgue carried with him from Paris to Germany, there was scarcely a hint, for example, of his distant childhood in South America, of the atmosphere of Tarbes in southern France where he had grown up, or of his later teenage years in Paris where he was sent to finish his education. When there are lines in poems which seem to refer to the provincial town and the forests which surrounded it, or to city districts and their distinctively urban sounds and activities, these mainly occur as images or metaphors for states of mind, feelings, fleeting perceptions, or else are a mosaic of seeming actuality from which the more immediate, verbal actuality of a poem is created. Except for ambivalent metaphors where there seems to be a description or referential element even when the reader knows perfectly well that the metaphor's main function has to do with a state of mind, Laforgue rarely wrote a poem whose validity could be tested by or against ordinary experience. Art for him was distinct from life. It had to do with the mind, the imagination. Poems were not about things, they were.

He did not immediately discover how to make such a poem. At first he thought that his ideas about human existence were themselves poetic ideas, that imaginative insight and irony were virtually identical, and that to reject generally accepted social values was itself a sufficient guarantee that his poems would be original. Convinced of this, he wrote a large number of poems he called 'philosophical'. In this category are not just the poems in *Le Sanglot de la Terre*, as published by Jean-Aubry in Volume I of the second Mercure de France edition, but also the twelve poems first published in the magazine *la Guêpe* and republished by J. L. Debauve in his *Les Pages de 'la Guêpe'* and the fifty-seven previously unpublished poems which appeared for the first time in Pascal Pia's *Poésies complètes*. For a newcomer to Laforgue who is interested in these early poems, which the poet later suppressed, Pia's volume is essential because the two sections, 'Poèmes posthumes divers' (pp. 313–72) and 'Poèmes inédits' (pp. 373–472), constitute everything in verse that Laforgue is known to have written before the publication of *Les Complaintes*, or at least before he sent what he thought was his final copy of *Les Complaintes* to his publisher in Paris.

All this means that a useful way to approach *Les Complaintes* is to see why Laforgue so quickly rejected his 'philosophical' poems, because the difficulty he had in distinguishing between ideas and states of mind, between opinions and perceptions, was only resolved in the later poems. At first he wrote as though his ideas about the universe were themselves poetic insights which only had to be written down in post-Baudelairian alexandrines for them to be poems. Not unnaturally he believed the type of thing he thought he understood was intrinsically significant, exciting, poetic. The idea that peoples' lives were determined by biological necessities beyond their comprehension, that moral values were make-believe, that religion was fantasy nurtured by the need for succour and that a man's life, like the world as a whole, was essentially meaningless seemed so important in itself, in face of massive bourgeois optimism and complacency, that a poem had to be a real poem if it were faithful to these Nihilist verities. So he believed. A frequently quoted prose note from *Mélanges posthumes* shows the way Laforgue was thinking about poetry in 1881 and 1882.

MES LIVRES. —Œuvre de littérature et œuvre de prophète des temps nouveaux.

Un volume de vers que j'appelle philosophiques. Sans prétention. Naïvement. Je croyais. Puis, brusque déchirement. Deux ans de solitude dans les bibliothèques, sans amour, sans amis, la peur de la mort. Des nuits à méditer dans une atmosphère de Sinaï. Alors je m'étonne que les philosophes qui exécutent quotidiennement l'idée de la justice, les idoles religieuses, et métaphysiques, et morales soient si peu émus, à croire qu'ils ne sont pas persuadés de l'existence de ces choses. Puis, étonnement qu'il y ait dans notre génération de poètes si peu qui aient fait ce livre. Leconte de Lisle pas assez humain, trop élevé au sens bourgeois, Cazalis trop dilettante, Mme Ackermann pas assez artiste, pas

assez fouillée, Sully-Prudhomme trop froid, trop technique, et les autres
l'accidentel, seulement. Et alors je fais naïvement ce livre—cinq
parties—*Lamma sabachtani, Angoisses, Les poèmes de la mort, Les poèmes du
spleen, Résignations*: l'histoire, le journal d'un parisien de 1880, qui
souffre, doute et arrive au néant et cela dans le décor parisien, les
couchants, la Seine, les averses, les pavés gras, les Jablochkoff, et cela
dans une langue d'artiste, fouillée et moderne, sans souci des codes du
goût, sans crainte du cru, du forcené, des dévergondages cosmologiques,
du grotesque, etc.
    Ce livre sera intitulé: Le Sanglot de la terre. Première partie: ce
seront les sanglots de la pensée, du cerveau, de la conscience de la terre.
Un second volume où je concentrerai toute la misère, toute l'ordure de
la planète dans l'innocence des cieux, les bacchanales de l'histoire, les
splendeurs de l'Asie, les orgues de barbarie de Paris, le carnaval des
Olympes, la Morgue, le Musée Dupuytren, l'hôpital, l'amour, l'alcool,
le spleen, les massacres, les Thébaïdes, la folie, la Salpêtrière.[1]

This passage, and there are several passages like it both in
Mélanges posthumes and in Laforgue's correspondence, has a dis-
tinct genetic relationship to *Les Complaintes*. From these sets of
ideas were generated both the unsuccessful poems of *Le Sanglot de
la Terre* and the successful poems of *Les Complaintes*. Sets of ideas
they have to be called, because they were as unstable as the
doctrines and creeds they replaced. The young Laforgue assoc-
iated his own loneliness with what he regarded as the logical
impossibility of belief; his own misery with what he took to be
the misery of the planet; his own boredom with the meaning-
lessness of existence. Some of these associations or sets of ideas
were arbitrary. Why should he care about the 'filth of the planet'
or the 'baccanalia of history', if it was all in any case mean-
ingless? The relationship of intellectual scepticism to a type of
moral indignation is hardly convincing. Similarly, what is the
importance of a 'diary of a Parisian in 1880, who suffers, doubts
and arrives at Nothingness' if suffering and doubting do in fact
lack significance of any kind? Here, something extremely emo-
tional, 'suffering', is confusingly connected with something coldly
intellectual, 'the necessity of disbelief'. It does not take the
reader long to realize that Laforgue's position, like the position
of any other Nihilist, is logically untenable but this realization
serves to remind him of the obvious, which is that a man
alienated from the practical world of actions, decisions, choices,

and human relationships necessarily constructs his internal world from his mere observation of the external, making this construct his only reality. This Laforgue did, but without realizing immediately that a trust in the internally constructed world of the imagination was not consistent with having ideas *about* the external world. The alienated sensibility cannot logically indulge in social comment.

These remarks are not made for the sake of showing that Laforgue, in following Hartmann and Schopenhauer, had thought his way into an intellectual *cul-de-sac*. During the many years between Descartes and Sartre this particular *cul-de-sac* has been densely populated. Rather, the point is to perceive why Laforgue wrote *Le Sanglot de la Terre* and why he then rejected it. Most of the poems in *Le Sanglot de la Terre*, as well as most of the other poems that were written at the same time, are verse versions of the sentiment expressed in the quoted passage from *Mélanges posthumes*. To understand why Laforgue found these verse philosophizings so unsatisfactory is to appreciate more clearly the artistic challenge this particular Nihilist poet faced when he began to think about *Les Complaintes*. He wrote them rather as an adolescent who believes in the importance of his own doubts and questionings. He rejected them when he realized that such ideas were unsubtle, unsophisticated. That is to say, he may not have grown out of his conviction that a 'philosophical' appreciation of man's predicament took precedence over all other matters that might concern a person of intelligence, but he did realize that there was something unimaginative, even unattractive in a straightforward assertiveness. Thus, the question arose—what type of poem was appropriate, artistically, for his state of mind? In biographical terms this shift away from adolescent dogmatism to something more circumspect, from earnestness to a preference for pose—like the pose of a dandy or a dilettante, may not have had anything to do with Laforgue's writing at all. It may have been Augusta's household, or the Empress herself, who taught him to avoid the unsubtle. In literary terms, though, this shift involved considerable rethinking. By what means could he be faithful to his own Nihilist, anarchist, determinist vision of existence and yet write a poem of originality, a poem that did justice to his wit and immense facility with the language? Interestingly, his search for an answer took him, not to the work of contemporary French poets, for in 1881 he knew nothing of Verlaine, Rimbaud, Corbière, but to contemporary painting, about which he knew a great deal.

By far the most important element of Laforgue's life, as he prepared for the writing of *Les Complaintes*, was this interest in art, particularly sculpture and painting. Art was all that mattered. Work, finance, the professions, government did not matter. Art was only genuine if divorced from daily life and politics. That there was a widening gap between what satisfied the sensibilities of the few and the quality of life of the many was not of concern to a person like Laforgue. He consciously accepted an elitist position.[2] Such a gap could not be of concern since it was not perceived. The days in which rapid communication and a highly organized bureaucracy were to translate the facts of people's existence into social awareness and social policy had not yet arrived. This meant that it was more common for a man to define his world in intellectual terms than in terms of social responsibility, in terms of books rather than knowledge, for example, of the community of which he was part. Books and ideas about books, painting, sculpture were accessible; the life of France—except for the conventional organizations of law and local government—could not be imagined. Anyone interested in art did not wish to imagine it. Why should such a person concern himself with social injustice in Marseilles or labour problems in the north-east when the highest achievements of civilization could be enjoyed and appreciated in the Louvre or in the museum at Dresden, when there was a greater exchange of ideas in a single evening in a Parisian café or studio than could be detected in a provincial centre in a whole year? Art for art's sake made sense in this context. It made sense for the young Laforgue who, like many of his contemporaries, was alienated from the world of actuality. No apology had to be made for devoting energy to the understanding of art, least of all at a time when artistic values seemed more stable, more permanent and more interesting than political ones.

It was only natural, then, that in 1880 or thereabouts Laforgue should turn to art, and pictorial art in particular, as a location for his own imaginative life. He had the example of his contemporaries. He had the more immediate example of his brother, Emile, who was a student at the Ecole des Beaux-Arts and of his friends, the members of the 'Club des Hydropathes', who lived the café life and talked incessantly of anarchy, *avant-garde* poetry, the latest books, the latest theories. The influence of Taine's lectures at the Ecole des Beaux-Arts, and of his books, was strong both as the impressive work of a man who had thought about the meaning of art in universal terms and as an advocate of ideas about the social utility of art that Laforgue felt had to be strongly resisted. Charles Ephrussi, for whom Laforgue worked before going to Germany, was also a powerful force in his life. A blandly sophisticated and civilized immigrant from Eastern Europe, Ephrussi was a successful art critic who eventually, after Laforgue's death, became editor and then director of the *Gazette des Beaux-Arts.* He encouraged Laforgue in his study of art, informal though it was, and later created the channel by which he could submit articles and reviews to the *Gazette.* Equally important, perhaps, was the fact that Laforgue worked for a year in Ephrussi's house, surrounded by books and paintings,—in an atmosphere, in short, in which art was seen to be taken seriously. Very different, all this, from the life of a provincial centre like Tarbes.

Naturally enough, much of what Laforgue did in the early eighties under Ephrussi's influence did not relate to the writing of *Les Complaintes.* He did not immediately discover his own direction. His studies in Paris were of conventional, or traditional, art. They were naturally, inevitably based on the principal National collections. In Germany, too, he necessarily interested himself in what had already been accepted, to the extent that museums and public galleries reflected this. A budding art critic cannot readily ignore what most people like or what most people take for granted. But there was an important exception to this: Impressionism. The newly-worked-out attitude to poetry which resulted in the writing of *Les Complaintes* derived directly not simply from the fact that Laforgue appreciated Impressionist painting but from his rapidly achieved understanding of the principles of Impressionism. Impressionist art was a type of knowledge, a way of seeing the world, and it was Laforgue's way too.

Recent exhibitions celebrating the centenary of the first Impressionist Exhibition in 1874, in their emphasis on the brief period after the Franco-Prussian War and the Commune when Renoir, Pissarro, Sisley and Monet worked together, have tended to convey the idea that, historically, Impressionism was a phenomenon of the seventies, an idea which is consolidated by important collections, like that of the Jeu de Paume, and by the fact that many of the painters who identified themselves with the early Impressionist exhibitions turned away from Impressionist principles later on in their careers. But if more correctly understood, it becomes obvious that Impressionism did not really exist in the public mind until the early eighties. Considering that the influence of the Salon was still strong and that the new generation of painters could only present their works in annual exhibitions, it was quite natural that a decade should pass between the launching of a new theory of art and even modest acceptance of it. That acceptance was marked by Durand-Ruel's one man shows of the work of Monet, Pissarro, and Sisley[3] in the spring of 1883 in Paris (the first time these painters had exhibited separately) and, for Laforgue, by Durand-Ruel's exhibition of Impressionist painting in Berlin, also in 1883 (the first public exhibition of French Impressionist work in Germany).

Several years before this, however, Laforgue had recorded something of his own personal experience of Impressionist painting. In a letter to Ephrussi written from Germany in 1882, he recalled the room in Ephrussi's house in which he used to work:

Surtout les heures passées à travailler seuls dans votre chambre où éclatait la note d'un fauteuil jaune.—Et les impressionnistes! Deux éventails de Pissarro bâtis solidement par petites touches patientes.—De Sisley, la Seine avec poteaux télégraphiques et ciel de printemps. Une berge des environs de Paris avec un voyou bucolisant par les sentiers.— Et les pommiers en fleurs escaladant une colline, de Monet.—Et la sauvageonne ébouriffée de Renoir, et de Berthe Morisot un sous-bois profond et frais, une femme assise, son enfant, un chien noir, un filet à papillons. Et encore de Morisot, une bonne avec son enfant, bleu, vert, rose, blanc, soleil.—Et de Renoir encore, la Parisienne aux lèvres rouges en jersey bleu. Et cette très capricieuse femme au manchon, une rose laque à la boutonnière, dans un fond spirituellement fouetté de neige. Et la danseuse de Mary Cassatt en jaune vert blond roux, fauteuils rouges, nu [*sic*] des épaules. Et les danseuses nerveuses de Degas, et le Duranty de Degas—et le Polichinelle de Manet avec les vers de Banville![4]

By contrast to the quite evidently genuine pleasures expressed here is the sort of note Laforgue made on the annual Salon:

> Impression générale du Salon: usine crapuleuse, psychologie de mélodrame, d'Eden théâtre. Ciels sans conscience, esthétique de commis.[5]

In short, Laforgue, perhaps more than a handful of his contemporaries, had an early opportunity to appreciate Impressionist art. How specifically can this be demonstrated? To be precise about what Laforgue knew and admired is difficult. He certainly knew Monet's *La Grenouillère* for he referred to it many times: David Arkell thinks this painting by itself may have been the basis of Laforgue's theories about Impressionism.[6] In the same way, he referred once or twice to Pissarro's *Marché St. Martin*.[7] Laforgue's friends in Berlin, the Bernsteins (Bernstein was Ephrussi's cousin) owned a number of Manets, including *Marine* (1869), *Roses, Tulipes et Lilas blanc* (1880), *Pêches* (1882), *L'Homme au Chapeau Rond* (1882), *Lilas blancs* (1882) and *Bouquet de Pivoines* (1883).[8] In 1881, Sisley, having moved out of Paris and then in the middle of his brilliant Veneux-Nadon period, exhibited fourteen paintings in the offices of *La Vie moderne* at 7 Boulevard des Italiens. The show was not a financial success but, if Laforgue visited it, as he probably did, he saw more Sisleys in one place than anyone in the twentieth century (except of course for the Jeu de Paume collection of Sisley's earlier work). The catalogue of the 1883 Gurlitt exhibition, already mentioned, lists figure paintings by Manet, Renoir, Degas and Morisot, and landscapes by Monet, Boudin, Sisley and Pissarro. In short, Laforgue had himself seen a rather large number of Impressionist paintings, at exactly the point in time when several of the Impressionists were doing their strongest work. The paintings left their mark on his imagination. Yet it was not only the paintings that affected Laforgue, but also the theory of art which they implied. This means that, though he liked the work of Manet, Pissarro and Morisot, it was the work of Monet[9] and Sisley that actually influenced him most.

Amongst other things, and this occurred exactly when he was committing himself seriously to *Les Complaintes* in 1883, he found he wanted to write an article on Impressionism and in fact devoted about a year to it. He had started work at least by February 1883[10] and in the same month he wrote back to Henry for Théodore Duret's little book called *Les Peintres Impressionnistes* (Paris, 1878). When, or even if, he finished is uncertain, though in December he told Ephrussi: 'J'ai fait un assez long article de revue, une explication physiologique esthétique de la formule impressionniste que M. Bernstein traduisait pour une revue'.[11] This article, not surprisingly, he said would be compatible with 'L'Inconscient de Hartmann, le transformisme de Darwin, les travaux de Helmholtz'.

Laforgue, by 1881, was acquainted with the theoretical or critical writing of Zola,[12] Huysmans,[13] and Ephrussi.[14] In writing about the 1880 Impressionist Exhibition, Ephrussi had prepared the way for a greater public understanding of Impressionism by acknowledging, despite his own conservatism of taste, that there was a difference between 'puérile ambition' (i.e. a childish search for originality) and what he called 'l'effort sérieux et persévérant de la manie bizarre!' His account of what the Impressionists actually did evidently hit home as far as Laforgue was concerned:

Composer son tableau, non dans l'atelier, mais sur place, en présence du sujet se débarrasser de toute convention; se mettre en face de la nature et l'interpréter sincèrement, brutalement, sans se préoccuper de la manière officielle de voir; traduire scrupuleusement l'impression, la sensation, toute crue, tout étrange qu'elle puisse paraître; présenter l'être, vivant de geste et d'attitude, remuant, dans l'atmosphère et la lumière fugitives et toujours changeantes; saisir au passage l'incessante mobilité de la coloration de l'air; négliger à dessein les tons particuliers pour atteindre une unité lumineuse dont les éléments divers se fondent dans un ensemble indécomposable et arrivent par les dissonances mêmes à l'harmonie générale; faire en sorte que les figures soient inséparables des fonds, qu'elles en soient comme la résultante, et que, pour goûter l'œuvre, il faille l'embrasser dans son entier et la regarder à la distance voulue; tel est l'idéal de la nouvelle école.[15]

This was a solid and correct statement, all the more significant for its having come from a careful, conservative person like

Ephrussi, so much so that one might wonder at first what Laforgue might add to it, or indeed what anyone might add.

The answer to this probably lies in the interest in neurology that was shared by Laforgue and his friend, Charles Henry. Laforgue's attitude was more 'scientific'. He was interested, as were so many of his contemporaries, in the *process* of seeing, in the fundamental truth of what a man saw for himself as opposed to what he might experience at second hand. Once again, this truth was not an absolute truth: it was simply the most that a man could experience, the most that he could accept:

> Pour le monde de l'œil, dans les jouissances optiques d'un tableau vraiment optique, bien que les fibres optiques puissent être consultées uniquement en elles-mêmes, pour être complet, étudier aussi la variabilité d'intensités et de rythmes des jouissances optiques l'apport dans la jouissance des autres centres jouisseurs voisins—bien-être et malaise—comme pour les odeurs et les saveurs, l'état de chaud ou de froid, d'à jeun ou de satieté, fibrilles olfactives, papilles quotatives, tactiles, etc.[16]

Or, as he says in the same note, the artist and the critic, the poet and the reader should accept life as it is, its struggles, hesitations, conflicts, deceptions, desires, and not struggle against it, or idealize. Behind every thing is 'Le principe anarchique, concurrence vitale et sélection naturelle', which means, in Laforgue's opinion, that art is only legitimate if it accommodates this anarchy: 'tout ce qui constitue la vie doit constituer la vibration esthétique—de même que dans l'amour qu'on a pour une femme, du sale, du caractériste, de l'utilitaire, des déceptions, des nostalgies etc.'. Such an acceptance in turn means the rejection of the canons of classical taste, balance, composition, unity and so forth.

> La Vie, la vie et encore rien que la vie, c'est-à-dire le nouveau. Faites de la vie vivant telle quelle, et laissez le reste, vous êtes sûr de ne pas vous tromper.[17]

The aesthetic principles underlying Impressionist paintings and Laforgue's *Les Complaintes* were identical.[18] In each case, the starting point was the rejection of absolute standards and the acceptance of the idea that experience was relative, arbitrary, ephemeral, uncertain, though at certain moments, moments of intensified perception, extremely 'interesting'. This was consistent with the conviction that a man's internal response to external experiences was more significant than his actions in the external world, since those actions had no significance whatsoever. One of the images that Laforgue used for this was the 'clavier': a man was simply a musical instrument, a unique instrument, on which existence happened to play in a certain fashion. This experience he called 'legitimate' because, though it lacked absolute significance, it had actually happened to the individual concerned. It was his life. As a consequence, Laforgue could accept, and evidently accepted with great pleasure, the unheroic world of Renoir and Monet, the world of the café, the terrace, the theatre, the street, turning away from the manufacture of an art which emulated the classics:

> En art il s'agit d'être intéressant. Les coulisses de l'Opéra sont plus artistes que tous les phalanstères rêvés par Fourier. La morale n'a rien à voir avec l'art pur pas plus qu'avec l'amour pur.
>
> Une vieille civilisation décadente, l'humanité de Balzac, l'art japonais, les gladiateurs de Rome, Messaline, est-ce moins intéressant en art qu'une civilisation équilibrée, le siècle de Périclès... ?
>
> Moi, créature éphémère, un éphémère m'intéresse plus qu'un héros absolu, de même que moi, homme habillé, une créature en toilette éphémère m'intéresse plus qu'un modèle nu sculptural. Pour moi, humain, créature incomplète et éphémère, un impassible ravagé comme Leconte de Lisle, un corrompu nostalgique se débattant dans le fini, est plus intéressant—est plus mon frère—que Tiberge et tous les Desgenais...les uns sont des hypertrophiés, les autres des châtrés,—parce que jamais, Dieu en est témoin, la pauvre humanité n'a produit un *héros pur*, et que tous ceux qu'on nous cite dans l'antiquité sont des créatures comme nous, cristallisées en légendes,—ni Bouddha, ni Socrate, ni Marc-Aurèle,—je voudrais bien connaître leur vie quotidienne.
>
> Les êtres comme les civilisations hypertrophiés sont plus intéressants que les êtres, les civilisations équilibrées. Il s'agit de n'être pas médiocre. Il faut être un nouveau. Oui, le degré de bienfaisance est un critérium en morale, non en art, l'artiste étant un solitaire, un hypertrophié, de Shakespeare à Michel-Ange.[19]

This being his position, he wanted an art which was without rhetoric, that is without false posing, and which did justice to the plain fact of things as they were, things as they were observed to be.

If you ask *how* this shall be done, how will life be seized at the moment of intense perception, intense insight, intense direct experience of the external world, the answer for Laforgue at least is Impressionism.

> Où l'académique ne voit que le dessin extérieur enfermant le modelé, il voit les réelles lignes vivantes sans forme géometrique mais bâties de mille touches irrégulières qui, de loin, établissent la vie... L'impressionniste voit et rend la nature telle qu'elle est, c'est-à-dire uniquement en vibrations colorées.[20]

An earlier reviewer of *Les Complaintes* obviously thought so. In a review published in *La République française* on 31 August 1885 the anonymous writer explicitly associated the book with 'mysticisme, alexandrinisme, schopenhauerisme' and Impressionism. Furthermore, he said that the language of Impressionism was 'une langue enfilant au petit bonheur des consonances imprévues et sans syntaxe presque les images les plus criardes et les mots les plus exotiques qu'on puisse glaner dans les troisièmes dessous du *Dictionnaire* de Littré.' Whether he was correct in associating what he calls 'Alexandrian' with the techniques of Impressionist painting may of course be a matter of dispute. The reviewer for *La République française* clearly thought there was a connection and the whole review is informed with the assumption. Here are the last three paragraphs, then, of the most significant of the early reviews:

> M. Jules Laforgue, qui renchérit sur le schopenhauerisme, trop bourgeois, en s'adonnant à la *Philosophie de l'inconscient*, de Hartmann, d'un mysticisme plus large et plus profond et d'un pessimisme moins vulgaire, a imaginé de reprendre, pour traduire ses conceptions poétiques, cette vieille forme populaire de la *complainte* à la métrique naïve, aux refrains touchants, forme qui correspond en musique à son congénère l'orgue de Barbarie. Hâtons-nous d'ajouter que l'orgue de Barbarie des Complaintes que voici n'a de populaire que le tour rythmique et quelquefois de vieux refrains empruntés et demeure un instrument très raffiné, capable de subtiles nuances psychologiques comme des derniers effets dans le métier du vers.
> En ne voyant en tout ceci qu'affaire de curiosité, de chinoiserie littéraire même, si l'on veut avoir d'un coup une idée de la nouvelle école poétique avec ses extravagances et ses maquillages juvéniles comme avec ses richesses de génération littéraire de demain, il faut lire

(c'est déchiffrer que nous dirions pour certaines pièces) ces 50 *com-plaintes*. L'auteur y chante un peu de tout, depuis l'éternal féminin jusqu'à la mort, en passant par les nostalgies et les spleens obligés. La langue, condensée à l'excès, jette le plus souvent de la poudre aux yeux, et de la plus saugrenue, mais rencontre parfois ça et là la formule nette et vive de l'observation contemporaine. Le métier du vers, qui est certes ce que le cénacle a produit de plus caractéristique, en bon comme en pire, est un pêle-mêle de rythmes et de rimes inédits où nombre de strophes profondes et personnelles sont à retenir. Le tout fait une œuvre d'une originalité un peu mêlée, mais des plus curieuses comme produit d'un certain moment et d'un certain milieu.

Ajoutons que l'*humour* qui circule dans ce volume nous conduirait volontiers à croire que l'auteur n'y est pas toujours dupe du sérieux de ses tours de force et de ses jongleries et s'amuse simplement à jeter ses gourmes. Cela et les originales qualités de langue et d'observation dont il fait preuve dans ses bonnes pages nous sont un sûr garant que lorsque la nouvelle école prendra sa place au soleil, après son aînée parnas-sienne, M. Jules Laforgue y aura contribué par de nouvelles poésies d'une tenue moins décadente et d'un idéal plus sérieusement moderne.[21]

Though François Ruchon attributed this article to Laforgue's old teacher in Tarbes, it is fairly clear that Laforgue wrote it himself. Jean-Aubry must have realized this when he said it had to the present 'passed' as an article by Théophile Delcassé: Daniel Grojnowski put the full case when he republished it in *La Revue d'histoire littéraire de France* in February 1970. Laforgue's account of his own book in this article, which he confessed to Gustave Kahn he had written ('que j'ai confectionné'), shows amongst other things that, even while he was striving to be 'original at all costs', his poems were nonetheless informed by a deliberately worked out and consciously held set of aesthetic ideas, ideas which he either derived from or found in Impressionist art. For a just appreciation of *Les Complaintes* this seems important. They are not merely free. They are not merely iconoclastic. On the contrary, they are deliberately worked, deliberately contrived, in a way Laforgue thought was consistent with a modern mode of consciousness. He did not want reality to be structured by the traditional literary forms any more than a painter wanted classical models to pre-determine the way in which he saw life. Rather, both poet and painter wanted the actual experience of reality—albeit momentary, ephemeral, transitory—to be expressed in works of art which themselves were analagous, in formal terms, to the fragmented, unreliable nature of experience. This is the basis of Laforgue's remarks in *La République française* which are so clear, surely, that they do not need to be repeated.

What was the literary equivalent of Impressionism for Laforgue? As Laforgue the critic thought about modern art what were the implications for Laforgue the poet? Broadly speaking, many of his poems began to make manifest a new freedom of expression both in their language and in their structure. The aesthetic and philosophical opinions Laforgue held at this time made it unlikely that any poem of his would have the structure of coherent logic or continuous narrative, because experience as he saw it was illogical and incoherent, or at least coherent only in limited, personal ways. By contrast, the essentially fractured nature of a poem like 'Complainte des Pianos qu'on entend dans les Quartiers aisés', with its physical stanza breaks, its contrapuntal effects as one poetic idea is momentarily left undeveloped while another is introduced, and its complementary ironies which leave so much unresolved as aspects of consciousness which do not reduce themselves into simple extractable meanings, is something which is now made visible on the page, is asserted by the very structure of the poem, is in fact a re-making of experience as the poet felt it rather than in terms of received opinion or conventional response. In other words, 'Complainte des Pianos qu'on entend dans les Quartiers aisés', and the other poems like it, have the shape of sets of associated ideas, insights, sense-impressions. There is no other truth than this highly fragmented truth, the poem asserts. In writing a poem, the poet need not hesitate to occupy himself with the ephemeral details of day by day existence, because it is these details that constitute the only existence he can know, so that they must be an essential part of the fabric of any poem. Furthermore, Laforgue's scepticism expressed itself in a habit of irony which in turn determined the structure of a poem. The conviction that there were no absolutes and that bourgeois verities were suspect involved an inversion of values. What other people thought important was for Laforgue trivial; what they thought trivial he considered important. Then again, he was habitually ironic about himself: 'mes grandes angoisses métaphysiques / Sont passées à l'état de chagrins domestiques.' It was this ironical habit of mind that permitted him to develop the same type of art as the Impressionist painters.

His scepticism also affected his attitude to language. Because Laforgue avoided rhetoric, that is the inherited rhetoric of a 'high style', with the same determination as he avoided heroic or Romantic ideas, the language of his poetry is of crucial significance. By language, one means particularly his feeling for individual words. Just as the single brush-stroke ('virgule') of the Impressionist painter was used to capture fleeting moments of perception, so the single word, considered precisely, analytically, was used by Laforgue to capture meanings latent in the language though at variance with normal usage. Of single words, examined by Laforgue with lexicographical precision, were startling combinations of words created. In doing this, Laforgue did not abuse the language. On the contrary, he was a diction-ary addict with a classical education, a special type of poet who made poems with words whose normal connotations he could only regard ironically, because he did not believe in the world in which that 'normal' usage had been established. Because normal usage was for this reason uninteresting, abnormal usage had to be the vehicle for decadent insight. Laforgue's notorious neo-logisms are obviously part of this, because they contribute to the surface tensions and disturbances which are one of the most striking features of a Laforgue poem. More important, though, are the metaphorical tensions that result from Laforgue's feeling for words.

Take for example the lines:

> Chacun son tour, il est temps que je m'émancipe,
> Irradiant des Limbes mon inédit type.

as typical of the way Laforgue worked. As in most good poems the main sense is determined by the context: 'Complainte du Fœtus de Poète' is about the birth of the poet—the literal birth. The context makes clear that emancipation is from the womb, a somewhat unconventional notion of childbirth. But already there is a tension between context and word. The literary conceit of the poet conscious of his progress through his mother's uterus is capped by the second line of the couplet which is characteristically inventive. Plain sense has obviously not been abandoned, for the meaning is clear. On the other hand, much of the pleasure of the line is verbal. As the poet falls into the world, he is first aware of his mother's body, but 'des Limbes' is primarily an ironical reference to the Catholic creed in which a human being falls into limbo. Normal usage is inverted. The ordinary person—'type', (where the pun is obvious)—who has just been born, is 'inédit', that is to say previously unpublished. This new publication lights up the world into which it has burst. The slightly unconventional syntactical arrangement of the 'units' of sense (i.e. 'Irradiant' and 'des Limbes' and 'mon inédit type') somewhat emphasizes the tension between them. But it is an intriguing tension. The reader is drawn into the line and remains interested in the relationship of its poetic ideas long after he has understood the main drift of the poem. This is typical of Laforgue and is an example of the particular way in which he can be called 'verbal'. 'Complainte du Fœtus de Poète' consists of verbal combinations of this kind. It can be seen that its textural effects are integral to its total imaginative effect, and are not merely decorative, just as the surface interest of an Impressionist painting is not decorative either, but is in fact an integral part of the painter's way of seeing the world. Some readers may condemn Laforgue's neologisms, ironies, decadent double meanings and surface witticisms because their overall effect is to destroy the stability of the language as most people use it. Others will see that the question does not need to be regarded with ultimate seriousness and that there is a type of sensibility that needs the technique of verbal, syntactical and structural fragmentation with which Laforgue experimented in this volume.

Whether Laforgue was uniformly successful in writing poems which satisfied this aesthetic is another matter, one which will be discussed in the critical commentaries. Obviously he was not uniformly successful and part of the reason for this was the piece-meal way in which the volume was assembled.

It took Laforgue three years to write, re-write and assemble *Les Complaintes* for the version that was eventually published in 1885. Though the poems were rarely out of his mind, the three periods of intensive work by which he brought the book by stages to its present state can be identified. To distinguish as clearly as possible between these three stages of composition turns out to be useful, critically, because *Les Complaintes* is such an unequal volume, containing many early poems that might well not have been included. The unevenness, and particularly the impact of the poorer poems at the beginning of the book, must have put off many a reader. It therefore seems worth attempting to put the matter straight by describing the way in which the book was written. Laforgue's correspondence, the *Agenda* for 1883 in which some poems are mentioned by name, the presentation copies to Marie Laforgue and Laurent Tailhade in which Laforgue dated and located some poems, and the surviving proofsheets, taken together, allow a reconstruction in broad outline of the way in which the book was put together. They show that the book was first sent to Léon Vanier late in 1883; that Laforgue revised it and added further poems in the early summer of 1884; and that in 1885, when Gustave Kahn acting on Laforgue's behalf persuaded Vanier not to delay any longer, Laforgue added poems, made substantial changes at the proof stage, and even added further poems after the first set of proofs had been returned. All this amounted to a continuous process of emendation, or rather a continuously creative process which only ended when the book at last appeared.

Back in Berlin in the autumn of 1882 after his summer vacation in Tarbes, he at first found himself disinclined to write. 'Qu'il y a long-temps que je n'ai fait des vers! Faire des vers est un vieux préjugé. Na!'[22] But a month later he announced to Charles Henry that he had after all started to work:

Je travaille. Je me remets à faire des vers. Je vieux publier (mais pour donner seulement pour mes amis que mes choses intéressent et que cela pourra distraire) un petit volume de poésies toutes neuves qui s'appelleront: *Complaintes de la Vie* ou *le Livre des Complaintes*. Ce sera des complaintes lamentables rimées à la diable...[23]

He said he had written five. That was in November. Though he sometimes wondered whether this new volume might in the end have to be abandoned just as his first had been, he continued to work and as usual enjoyed it. 'Je travaille la nuit à la lampe.

C'est une infinie volupté. Toute la maison est endormie.'[24] Of course it was not only at his poems that he worked while the rest of the household slept. He still took his formal art criticism seriously and, judging by an *Agenda* entry, he at some point during the winter wrote a play. By the same token, he re-read Heine, Schopenhauer, Tolstoy, Dostoevsky during this period and no doubt much more that went unrecorded. But the type of poem he had begun to write possessed him, so much so that between Christmas 1882 and the end of the summer period at Baden-Baden in 1883 he completed the volume—that is to say, the first version of it.

Undoubtedly his affair with the woman designated only by the letter R in the *Agenda* (a Laforgue mystery which has still to be solved) had an impact upon the poems, particularly in the spring and early summer of 1883 when their seeing each other frequently coincided with a highly creative period in which a good proportion of the poems must have been written. In February and March, still in Berlin, they went to plays, concerts, and exhibitions together, including Ambroise Thomas's production of *Hamlet* and Durand-Ruel's exhibition of French Impressionist paintings at Gurlitt's gallery. On 19 March is the first entry of the name of a 'Complainte', the 'Complainte du Fœtus'. Unpublished prose notes, as well as some of the poems (such as 'Complainte d'un certain Dimanche') suggest, and the *Agenda* tends to confirm, that Laforgue and R from time to time exchange the tedium of the court for anonymous weekends in hotels. The mention of the Hôtel de Rome in the *Agenda* entry for 14 April probably means this, and they seem not to have travelled by the directest route when they went to Baden in April and from Baden to Coblenz in May. In fact the second journey took ten days. From April onwards, *Agenda* entries which date the composition of particular poems are interspersed with entries about R, rarely more than two or three words and perhaps indicating little more than that they were getting on with each other or that they were not. So 'promenade avec R' on 15 April is followed by 'chez R scène interminable' the next day. Visiting Dresden for the sake of its museum on their roundabout route to Baden, Laforgue seems reconciled: 'bout de Tendresse, serrement de mains tièdes avec R' but then for several days there were what he called 'scènes'. Once in Baden, Laforgue worked hard, as was to become his habit in the years which followed and the hard work coincided with a rapid strengthening of the friendship. The pattern of existence was something disturbed, as on 27 May when he made the longest of all the entries! 'Grande scène avec R...Elle était née pour être mère'. But life went on. They continued to see a lot of each other, played croquet in public and in private enjoyed their 'weekending'. How serious it all was is hard to judge. Some of the entries seem juvenile, such as his note on having tea on the train to Coblenz with R and her friends: 'R se pressait contre moi'. On the other hand, if the entry for 22 July 1883 is associated with 'Complainte d'un certain Dimanche', that weekend at least must have been serious enough.

Meanwhile, the volume was shaping itself as he wrote. Early in May, he had twenty poems and felt confident enough to tell his sister, Marie, what he was doing. 'Je trouve stupide de faire la grosse voix et de jouer d'éloquence. Aujourd'hui que je suis plus sceptique et que je m'emballe moins aisément et que, d'autre part, je possède ma langue d'une façon plus minutieuse, plus clownesque, j'écris de petits poèmes de fantaisie, n'ayant qu'un but: faire de l'original à tout prix. J'ai la *ferme intention* de publier un tout petit volume (jolie édition), luxe typographique, écrin digne de mes bijoux littéraires! titre: *Quelques complaintes de la vie*.'[25] By the middle of July he said he had between 30 and 40, meaning then that he was thinking about which poems to include in the volume. By the end of July he had finished. He announced this in a letter to Charles Henry[26] and on 2 August made the *Agenda* entry: 'Fermé mes complaintes'. When he went to Paris on the way to Tarbes for his summer vacation he took the poems with him.

Whether he had a chance to read them to his Paris friends in August, whether he made any attempt then to find a publisher, difficult as that would have been in the holidays, whether he further revised the poems during his weeks in Tarbes—these things are unknown. Perhaps he did revise them, because some months were to pass before he asked Henry to help him find a publisher. Laforgue wanted an elegant volume and yet could not afford to pay very much for it so the search took time. At least one of the publishers approached by Henry, Alphonse Lemerre, proved too expensive. Eventually, Laforgue settled on Léon Vanier, a new and relatively unknown publisher who was only just beginning to make a name for himself as a publisher of *avant-garde* verse. In February he wrote to Henry: 'Ne vaut-il pas mieux s'adresser à cet idéal Léon Vanier sur le quai avant d'arriver à Notre-Dame, Léon Vanier qui imprime sur un divin papier d'épicerie des vers de Verlaine, Valade, etc.... On lui commanderait une édition, le moins d'exemplaires possible, de 3e classe (comme aux pompes funèbres) et on lui donnerait 300 frs en juillet'.[27] Poor Laforgue thought that his poems would be published quickly. When he sent the manuscript to Charles Henry in November, he told Kahn that his volume—'tout flambant neuf et très éteint'—would appear in February.[28] Luckily for his spirits, he did not then know that two and a half years were to pass before the book finally appeared.

Amongst the letters from Laforgue to Vanier in the possession of J. L. Debauve is one dated 14 March 1884,[29] in which Laforgue agreed to the terms Vanier had proposed, that is, that Laforgue would pay an advance of 200 francs on 1 July for an edition of 500 copies. 'Le manuscrit tel que vous l'avez reçu est définitif', he told Vanier with unjustified optimism.[30] Because he had agreed to pay for the poems at the beginning of July, he expected the proofs in June.[31] They did not arrive. As Debauve has shown, Vanier was busy with other books and, since he used just the one printer, not everything could be done at once; Laforgue's book could hardly have enjoyed a high priority.

Laforgue himself was not unoccupied. 'Le Vanier a raison d'attendre, et puis je pourrai revoir la chose et supprimer des grossièretés qu'une vulgaire conception de la force en littérature (l'éloquence! tords-lui le cou, comme dit Verlaine) m'avait induit à y laisser'.[32] In other words he was prepared to pretend that he did not mind the delay, or at least that he could accept it, and meanwhile the process of correction and re-writing continued. The changes Laforgue continued to make to the text and the delays in Paris which Vanier made little attempt to justify in the end converted this into a minor classic of author-publisher relationships. 'Et les épreuves de mes complaintes?' Laforgue asked Vanier six months later. 'J'espère que maintenant que me voilà hors de Paris et de France vous ne me considérez pas pour cela comme lointain et perdu et mythique et par conséquent comme indéfiniment négligeable?'[33] 1884 had somehow slipped by and it was not until Gustave Kahn took up the cudgels on Laforgue's behalf early in 1885 that Vanier stirred himself.

The spring of 1885 saw a new burst of activity as at last the poems went to press and Laforgue yet again had a reason for thinking about them. When Kahn asked about them, he replied that Vanier had given assurances that they would appear in December—that is, December 1884, and Kahn was so shocked that he offered his help.[34] By February Kahn had begun to make progress and Laforgue thanked him for his good offices. 'Que je te remercie très vivement pour toutes tes courses délicates chez Vanier. Tu combats le bon combat. Cela me dit aussi que tu approuves le titre et les épigraphes...Penses-tu comme le mathématicien du coin que je doive sacrificier cette *alleluia-préface* qui me semble à moi servir si passablement de toile de fond avec son air enfant et passé?'[35] The practical problems at this stage were Laforgue's desire to retain the early 'philosophical' poem and his dislike of Vanier's monogram or imprint. On the first, he had to defend himself vigorously. He said that he wanted to keep the autobiographical preface to show people 'qu'avant d'être dilettante et pierrot j'ai sejourné dans le Cosmique'.[36] A little later he wrote: 'J'ai insisté aussi pour le maintien de ma préface qui est tout ce que je me permettrai du volume *des philosophes* d'avant ta Tunisie'.[37]

The proof reading, which began in March, turned out to be an extraordinary business. Two sets of proof sheets were produced, with a gap between them of three or four months, and in both instances Laforgue was sent two copies. One set of the first proofs was sent to Henry, who passed it on to Gustave Kahn, who then sent it with corrections to Laforgue. The other set was sent to Laforgue, who returned it before he knew his friend's comments.[38] The proofs reached him in batches and he not only corrected, but also revised and re-wrote as he went on. His being in Germany while the poems were being printed and his inexperience in publication matters are, of course, principal causes of the extreme messiness of the first edition text. He simply did not appreciate that if he wanted a beautiful book *he* as well as the printer had to be careful over details. Eventually he got himself into difficulty by expanding what he said was an important poem, 'Complainte des Voix sous le Figuier bouddhique', which resulted in disruption of the page proofs and the need to reset the first four gatherings. It was also at the proof stage that he added an additional poem, and a few days later added two more. Laforgue realized that he would probably have to pay for these luxuries. 'Je vous renvoie ces épreuves. Vous verrez que j'ai beaucoup ajouté à la pièce *les voix etc.* pour moi la plus importante (significative) en un sens du volume—J'ai numéroté la série des distiques pour l'ordre dans lequel il seront placés.— J'espère qu'on se tirera d'affaire. Une erreur dans cette pièce me désolerait.—Maintenant il est franchement entendu que si ce supplément de correction doit être à ma charge. Je trouverais tout naturel que vous me fassiez une petite note de cela, car j'aurai peut-être quelques autres menues additions à faire (mais j'en doute autant que je me souvienne) au reste des épreuves.'[39] Hardly words to delight a publisher's ear.

In April he told Vanier to place the three additional poems at the end, to make up a round fifty!

The poems were published on 25 July 'en bleu et en vert' and Laforgue asked for a dozen copies to be sent to him in Germany, so that he could present them to his friends and family, including Henry, Gautier-Villars, Jacques-Emile Blanche, Marie Laforgue, Laurent Tailhade and J.-K. Huysmans.[40] There seems to be no record of what he thought of the volume when he received it, nor did he talk with any of his friends (or write to them at least) about the significance of the way in which the book had been assembled. The other book prepared for publication in 1885 was eventually given the title *L'Imitation de Notre-Dame la Lune 1881– 6*, the dates providing tacit acknowledgement that, though the Pierrot poems were at the centre of the volume, earlier poems had been used to fill it out. A reader must decide for himself, since the question is purely a critical one, whether *L'Imitation de Notre-Dame la Lune* would have been a better book if it had only contained poems written in 1885 and 1886, and whether *Les Complaintes* would have been a better book if it had only contained the poems written during and after 1883. In the case of

Les Complaintes this question is discussed in some detail in the Commentaries to individual poems. Of course the poet must be governed by his own feelings about the internal coherence and integrity of a book when he makes it, but one cannot help feeling that this particular volume would have been better received if he had reduced it in size.

To what extent is it possible to relate this process of publication and revision to particular poems? And to what extent can the various groups of poems in the volume be distinguished from each other: that is, the poems written before 1882 but later revised, the poems written in 1883—the true year of the 'Complainte', and Laforgue's selection of those poems he had written in 1884 and 1885, which he added after the book had first been sent to Vanier? As mentioned earlier, only in part. Some poems were first written in 1880. Some, but not all, of these were revised in 1885. 'Préludes autobiographiques' was obviously one of these, while two of the three poems Laforgue sent to Vanier at the last moment in April 1885 were re-written versions of poems composed before Laforgue had conceived a volume called *Les Complaintes*. These were 'Complainte-Litanies de mon Sacré-Cœur' and 'Complaintes des Débats mélancoliques et littéraires'. Among the poems that cannot be dated with certainly there may be other fossils of this kind.

Laforgue's notes in his sister's copy date some of the earlier poems. 'Complaintes des Condoléances au Soleil' in 1881 and 'Complainte des Pubertés difficiles', 'Complainte de la Vigie aux Minuits polaires' and 'Complainte des grands Pins dans une Villa abandonnée' he said had been written in 1882. Here it must be remembered that, quite apart from the possibility that Laforgue's memory may not have served him faithfully, he was dating and locating the first writing of the poem, which may later have gone through several versions during the two year process of revision described above. This was the case, for example, with 'Complainte des grands Pins dans une Villa abandonnée'. In the copy he sent to his sister (who did not know about R) he wrote: 'Octobre 1882, boulevard Saint-Michel'. But there is also an *Agenda* entry for 20 May 1883 which would seem to indicate that he re-wrote the poem. A few of these earlier poems (in their earlier versions) can also be dated from the correspondence, as will be indicated in the Commentaries.

The poems mentioned by name in the *Agenda* for 1883 are the following:

19 March	Complainte du Fœtus
20 March	Complaintes des Amoureuses
22 March	Prologue à mes Complaintes
2 May	Complainte des Tapisseries de haute lisse
12 May	Complainte des Pianos
17 May	Complaintes des Bals
25 May	Complainte du Soir d'Hyménée
26 May	Complaintes des Aveugles.

Since some of these poems appear later with slightly different titles while some disappear, the list is more important as the evidence of a burst of creative activity than as a statement about particular poems. A few other poems, not mentioned in the *Agenda*, can be said with certainty to derive from 1883. One of these was 'Complainte d'un certain Dimanche' written in July 1883. Another was 'Complaintes des Cloches' written in Liège in August. When critical considerations are also taken into account, however, it becomes clear that about two-thirds of the poems were written during 1883, which was the year the book itself came into being.

It is interesting, nonetheless, to identify poems which were written in 1884, despite the critical dilemmas which arise when one compares an unrevised 1884 poem with a revised poem whose first version was written earlier. Poems written in 1884 include 'Complainte d'un autre Dimanche', 'Complainte de la Lune en Province' (written at Cassel in July), 'Grande Complainte de la Ville de Paris' (written in a hotel in the rue Madame in Paris in August) and 'Complainte-Variations sur le mot *falot, falotte*' (written at Chevreuse in August while he was on holiday with Henry). An earlier version of 'Complainte d'une Convalescence' was written in Coblenz in June, though whether that was the first version is not completely certain. It may well have been. Again, these matters are discussed in greater detail in the Commentaries on particular poems.

That the poems as published in the first edition were very different from the poems as first written is attested not only by the substantive changes to the proof but also by the slight manuscript evidence that has survived.[41] Laforgue warned Henry to be careful with the manuscript, since he had not kept a copy for himself. He meant a fair copy of course. J. L. Debauve possesses a manuscript of 'Complainte de la Fin des Journées' which he says is different, though not in any crucial sense, from the final version. Given the fact that the poems evolved in what was obviously an important formative as well as highly creative phase in Laforgue's writing career, it is a pity that study of the changes from version to version is impossible.

It must be mentioned finally that Léo Trézenick, the printer (whose real name, by the way, was Léon Epinette), extracted some of the poems while they were going through the press for serial publication in a magazine of his own, *La Lutèce*. Once Laforgue had recovered from his surprise, it appears he did not object. 'Complainte des Blackboulés' appeared in the issue dated 17–24 May 1885, followed by 'Complainte sur certains Temps déplacés' and 'Complainte des Condoléances au Soleil' in 21–8 June, and 'Complainte-Litanies de mon Sacré-Cœur' in 19–23 July.

So much for the process by which the book was made. Given the breaks, disruptions, confusions of the process, it is hardly to be expected that the book as published would have a readily detectable, internal, imaginative integrity. Nor does it. Laforgue's Nihilism is an informing principle and gives the volume a certain unity in that, whatever kind of poem he makes, whatever he writes about, it is imagined from the same point of view. His intellectual and imaginative premises never varied. Yet this remark applies equally to his other works as well: *L'Imitation de Notre-Dame la Lune*, *Moralités légendaires*, and *Derniers Vers*. What gives *Les Complaintes* its character is the exuberance and originality of technique—the sheer technical daring of the best poems, which will be analysed and discussed in some detail in the critical commentaries. By pure genius Laforgue had found for himself one of the escape routes from traditional prosody and the long-established notions of what a poem really was. Having done so, he wrote in 1883 a group of poems of quite extraordinary wit and vitality. Whether these poems are powerful, imaginative works over and above, or beyond, the technical virtuosity that characterizes them is a difficult question. A few undoubtedly are. In regarding Laforgue's career as a whole one tends to return to the obvious differences between *Les Complaintes*, where Laforgue's inventiveness provides so many moments of pure pleasure, and *Derniers Vers*, whose purposes are more profound and whose art is more mature. This is not to disparage *Les Complaintes*, however; only to suggest that they are best enjoyed when accepted for what they are: *les jeux d'esprit* of the Nihilist whose Littré disclosed a decadent, brilliantly contrived verbal and intellectual universe.

A Paul Bourget

En deuil d'un Moi-le-Magnifique
Lançant de front les cent pur-sang
De ses vingt ans tout hennissants,
Je vague, à jamais Innocent,
Par les blancs parcs ésotériques   5
De l'Armide Métaphysique.

Un brave bouddhiste en sa châsse,
Albe, oxydé, sans but, pervers,
Qui, du chalumeau de ses nerfs,
Se souffle gravement des vers,   10
En astres riches, dont la trace
Ne trouble le Temps ni l'Espace.

C'est tout. A mon temple d'ascète
Votre Nom de Lac est piqué:
Puissent mes feuilleteurs du quai,   15
En rentrant, se r'intoxiquer
De vos AVEUX, ô pur poëte!
C'est la grâce que je m'souhaite.

Préludes Autobiographiques

Soif d'infini martyre? Extase en théorèmes
Que la création est belle, tout de même!

En voulant mettre un peu d'ordre dans ce tiroir,
Je me suis perdu par mes grands vingt ans, ce soir
De Noël gras.
       Ah! dérisoire créature!
Fleuve à reflets, où les deuils d'Unique ne durent   5
Pas plus que d'autres! L'ai-je rêvé, ce Noël
Où je brûlais de pleurs noirs un mouchoir réel,
Parce que, débordant des chagrins de la Terre
Et des frères Soleils, et ne pouvant me faire
Aux monstruosités sans but et sans témoin   10
Du cher Tout, et bien las de me meurtrir les poings
Aux steppes du cobalt sourd, ivre-mort de doute,
Je vivotais, altéré de *Nihil* de toutes
Les citernes de mon Amour?

                   Seul, pur, songeur,   15
Me croyant hypertrophique! comme un plongeur
Aux mouvants bosquets des savanes sous-marines,
J'avais roulé par les livres, bon mysogine.

Cathédrale anonyme! en ce Paris, jardin
Obtus et chic, avec son bourgeois de Jourdain   20
A rêveurs; ses vitraux fardés, ses vieux dimanches
Dans les quartiers tannés où regardent des branches
Par dessus les murs des pensionnats, et ses
Ciels trop poignants à qui l'Angélus fait: assez!

Paris qui, du plus bon bébé de la Nature,   25
Instaure un lexicon mal cousu de ratures.

Bon breton né sous les Tropiques, chaque soir
J'allais le long d'un quai bien nommé *mon rêvoir,*
Et buvant les étoiles à même: 'ô Mystère!
'Quel calme chez les astres! ce train-train sur terre!   30
'Est-il Quelqu'un, vers quand, à travers l'infini,
'Clamer l'universel *lamasabaktani?*
'Voyons; les cercles du Cercle, en effets et causes,
'Dans leurs incessants vortex de métamorphoses,
'Sentent pourtant, abstrait, ou, ma foi, quelque part,   35
'Battre un cœur! un cœur simple; ou veiller un Regard!
'Oh! qu'il n'y ait personne et que Tout continue!
'Alors géhenne à fous, sans raison, sans issue!
'Et depuis les Toujours, et vers l'Eternité!
'Comment donc quelque chose a-t-il jamais été!   40
'Que Tout se sache seul au moins, pour qu'il se tue!
'Draguant les chantiers d'étoiles, qu'un Cri se rue,
'Mort! emballant en ses linceuls aux clapotis
'Irrévocables, ces sols d'impôts abrutis!
'Que l'Espace ait un bon haut-le-cœur et vomisse   45
'Le Temps nul, et ce Vin aux geysers de justice!
'Lyres des nerfs, filles des Harpes d'Idéal
'Qui vibriez, aux soirs d'exil, sans songer à mal,
'Redevenez plasma! Ni Témoin, ni spectacle!
'Chut, ultime vibration de la Débâcle,   50
'Et que Jamais soit Tout, bien intrinsèquement,
'Très hermétiquement, primordialement!'

Ah!—Le long des calvaires de la Conscience,
La Passion des mondes studieux t'encense,
Aux Orgues des Résignations, Idéal,   55
O Galathée aux pommiers de l'Eden-Natal!

Martyres, croix de l'Art, formules, fugues douces,
Babels d'or où le vent soigne de bonnes mousses;
Mondes vivotant, vaguement étiquetés
De livres, sous la céleste Eternullité: 60
Vanité, vanité, vous dis-je!—Oh! moi, j'existe,
Mais où sont, maintenant, les nerfs de ce Psalmiste?
Minuit un quart; quels bords te voient passer, aux nuits

Anonymes, ô Nébuleuse-Mère? Et puis,
Qu'il doit agoniser d'étoiles éprouvées, 65
A cette heure où Christ naît, sans feu pour leurs couvées,
Mais clamant: ô mon Dieu! tant que, vers leur ciel mort,
Une flèche de cathédrale pointe encor
Des polaires surplis!—Ces Terres se sont tues,
Et le création fonctionne têtue! 70
Sans issue, elle est Tout; et nulle autre, elle est Tout,
X en soi? Soif à trucs! Songe d'une nuit d'août?
Sans le mot, nous serons revannés, ô ma Terre!
Puis tes sœurs. *Et nunc et semper*, *Amen*. Se taire.

Je veux parler au Temps! criais-je. Oh! quelque engrais 75
Anonyme! Moi! mon Sacré-Cœur!—J'espérais
Qu'à ma mort, tout frémirait, du cèdre à l'hysope;
Que ce Temps, déraillant, tomberait en syncope,
Que, pour venir jeter sur mes lèvres des fleurs,
Les Soleils très navrés détraqueraient leurs chœurs; 80
Qu'un soir, du moins, mon Cri me jaillissant des moelles,
On verrait, mon Dieu, des signaux dans les étoiles?

Puis, fou devant ce ciel qui toujours nous bouda,
Je rêvais de prêcher la fin, nom d'un Bouddha!
Oh! pâle mutilé, d'un: qui m'aime me suive! 85
Faisant de leurs cités une unique Ninive,
Mener ces chers bourgeois, fouettés d'alléluias,
Au Saint-Sépulcre maternel du Nirvâna!
Maintenant, je m'en lave les mains (concurrence
Vitale, l'argent, l'art, puis les lois de la France...) 90

Vermis sum, pulvis es! où sont mes nerfs d'hier?
Mes muscles de demain? Et le terreau si fier
De Mon âme, où donc était-il, il y a mille
Siècles? et comme, incessamment, il file, file!...
Anonyme! et pour Quoi?—Pardon, Quelconque Loi! 95
L'être est forme, Brahma seul est Tout-Un en soi.

O Robe aux cannelures à jamais doriques
Où grimpent les Passions des grappes cosmiques;

O Robe de Maïa, ô Jupe de Maman,
Je baise vos ourlets tombals éperdument!   100
Je sais! la vie outrecuidante est une trève
D'un jour au Bon Repos qui pas plus ne s'achève
Qu'il n'a commencé. Moi, ma trève, confiant,
Je la veux cuver au sein de l'INCONSCIENT.

Dernière crise. Deux semaines errabundes,   105
En tout, sans que mon Ange Gardien me réponde.
Dilemne à deux sentiers vers l'Eden des Elus:
Me laisser éponger mon Moi par l'Absolu?
Ou bien, élixirer l'Absolu en moi-même?
C'est passé. J'aime tout, aimant mieux que Tout m'aime.   110
Donc Je m'en vais flottant aux orgues sous-marins,
Par les coraux, les œufs, les bras verts, les écrins,
Dans la tourbillonnante éternelle agonie
D'un Nirvâna des Danaïdes du génie!
Lacs de syncopes esthétiques! Tunnels d'or!   115
Pastel défunt! fondant sur une langue! Mort
Mourante ivre-morte! Et la conscience unique
Que c'est dans la Sainte Piscine ésotérique
D'un *lucus* à huis-clos, sans pape et sans laquais,
Que J'ouvre ainsi mes riches veines à Jamais.   120

En attendant la mort mortelle, sans mystère,
Lors quoi l'usage veut qu'on nous cache sous terre.

Maintenant, tu n'as pas cru devoir rester coi;
Eh bien, un cri humain! s'il en reste un pour toi.

Complainte Propitiatoire à l'Inconscient

Aditi.

O Loi, qui êtes parce que Vous Etes,
Que Votre Nom soit la Retraite!

—Elles! ramper vers elles d'adoration?
Ou que sur leur misère humaine je me vautre?   5
Elle m'aime, *infiniment*! Non, d'occasion!
Si non *moi*, ce serait *infiniment* un autre!

    Que votre inconsciente Volonté
    Soit faite dans l'Eternité!   10

—Dans l'orgue qui par déchirements se châtie,
Croupir, des étés, sous les vitraux, en langueur;
Mourir d'un attouchement de l'Eucharistie,
S'entrer un crucifix maigre et nu dans le cœur?

    Que de votre communion, nous vienne   15
    Notre sagesse quotidienne!

—O croisés de mon sang! transporter les cités!
Bénir la Pâque universelle, sans salaires!
Mourir sur la Montagne, et que l'Humanité,
Aux âges d'or sans fin, me porte en scapulaires?   20

    Pardonnez-nous nos offenses, nos cris,
    Comme étant d'à jamais écrits!

—Crucifier l'infini dans des toiles comme
Un mouchoir, et qu'on dise: 'Oh! l'Idéal s'est tu!'
Formuler Tout! En fugues sans fin dire l'Homme!   25
Etre l'âme des arts à zones que veux-tu?

Non, rien; délivrez-nous de la Pensée,
Lèpre originelle, ivresse insensée,

　Radeau du Mal et de l'Exil;
　　Ainsi soit-il.　　　　　　　　30

Complainte-Placet de Faust Fils

Si tu savais, maman Nature,
Comme Je m'aime en tes ennuis,
Tu m'enverrais une enfant pure,
        Chaste aux '*et puis*?'   4

Si tu savais quelles boulettes,
Tes soleils de Panurge! dis,
Tu mettrais le nôtre en miettes,
        En plein midi.   8

Si tu savais, comme la *Table*
De tes Matières est mon fort!
Tu me prendrais comme comptable,
        Comptable à mort!   12

Si tu savais! les fantaisies!
Dont Je puis être le ferment!
Tu ferais de moi ton Sosie,
        Tout simplement.   16

Complainte à Notre-Dame des Soirs

L'Extase du soleil, peuh! La Nature, fade
Usine de sève aux lymphatiques parfums.
Mais les lacs éperdus des longs couchants défunts
Dorlotent mon voilier dans leurs plus riches rades,
    Comme un ange malade...   5
    O Notre-Dame des Soirs,
    Que Je vous aime sans espoir!

Lampes des mers! blancs bizarrants! mots à vertiges!
Axiomes *in articulo mortis* déduits!
Ciels vrais! Lune aux échos dont communient les puits! 10
Yeux des portraits! Soleil qui, saignant son quadrige,
    Cabré, s'y crucifige!
    O Notre-Dame des Soirs,
    Certe, ils vont haut vos encensoirs!

Eux sucent des plis dont le frou-frou les suffoque; 15
Pour un regard, ils battraient du front les pavés;
Puis s'affligent sur maint sein creux, mal abreuvés;
Puis retournent à ces vendanges sexciproques.
    Et moi, moi Je m'en moque!
    Oui, Notre-Dame des Soirs, 20
    J'en fais, paraît-il, peine à voir.

En voyage, sur les fugitives prairies,
Vous me fuyez; ou du ciel des eaux m'invitez;
Ou m'agacez au tournant d'une vérité;
Or vous ai-je encor dit votre fait, je vous prie? 25
    Ah! coquette Marie,
    Ah! Notre-Dame des Soirs,
    C'est trop pour vos seuls Reposoirs!

Vos Rites, jalonnés de sales bibliothèques,
Ont voûté mes vingt ans, m'ont tari de chers goûts.   30
Verrai-je l'oasis fondant au rendez-vous,
Où...vos lèvres (dit-on!) à jamais nous dissèquent?
     O Lune sur La Mecque!
     Notre-Dame, Notre-Dame des Soirs,
     De *vrais* yeux m'ont dit: au revoir!   35

Complainte des Voix sous le Figuier bouddhique

LES COMMUNIANTES

Ah! ah!
Il neige des hosties
De soie, anéanties!
Ah! ah!
Alleluia!   5

LES VOLUPTANTES

La lune en son halo ravagé n'est qu'un œil
Mangé de mouches, tout rayonnant des grands deuils.

Vitraux mûrs, déshérités, flagellés d'aurores,
Les Yeux Promis sont plus dans les grands deuils encore.

LES PARANYMPHES

Les *concetti* du crépuscule   10
Frisaient les bouquets de nos seins;
Son haleine encore y circule,
Et, leur félinant le satin
Fait s'y pâmer deux renoncules.

Devant ce Maître Hypnotiseur,   15
Expirent leurs frou-frou poseurs;
Elles crispent leurs étamines,
Et se rinfiltrent leurs parfums
    Avec des mines
    D'œillets défunts.   20

LES JEUNES GENS

Des rêves engrappés se roulaient aux collines,
Feuilles mortes portant du sang des mousselines,

Cumulus, indolents roulis, qu'un vent tremblé
Vint carder un beau soir de soifs de s'en aller!

LES COMMUNIANTES

Ah! ah!   25
Il neige des cœurs
Noués de faveurs,
Ah! ah!
Alleluia!

LES VOLUPTANTES

Reviens, vagir parmi mes cheveux, mes cheveux   30
Tièdes, Je t'y ferai des bracelets d'aveux!

Entends partout les Encensoirs les plus célestes,
L'univers te garde une note unique! reste...

LES PARANYMPHES

C'est le nid meublé
Par l'homme idolâtre;   35
Les vents déclassés
Des mois près de l'âtre;
Rien de passager,
Presque pas de scènes;
La vie est si saine,   40
Quand on sait s'arranger.
O fiancé probe,
Commandons ma robe!
Hélas! le bonheur est là, mais lui se dérobe...

LES JEUNES GENS

Bestiole à chignon, Nécessaire divin,   45
Os de chatte, corps de lierre, chef-d'œuvre vain!

O femme, mammifère à chignon, ô fétiche,
On t'absout; c'est un Dieu qui par tes yeux nous triche.

Beau commis voyageur, d'une Maison là-haut,
Tes yeux mentent! ils ne nous diront pas le Mot!   50

Et tes pudeurs ne sont que des passes réflexes
Dont joue un Dieu très fort (Ministère des sexes).

Tu peux donc nous mener au Mirage béant,
Feu-follet connu, vertugadin du Néant;

Mais, fausse sœur, fausse humaine, fausse mortelle,   55
Nous t'écartèlerons de hontes sangsuelles!

Et si ta dignité se cabre? à deux genoux,
Nous te fermerons la bouche avec des bijoux.

—Vie ou Néant! choisir. Ah quelle discipline!
Que n'est-il un Eden entre ces deux usines?   60

   Bon; que tes doigts sentimentals
   Aient pour nos fronts au teint d'épave
   Des condoléances qui lavent
   Et des trouvailles d'animal.

   Et qu'à jamais ainsi tu ailles,   65
   Le long des étouffants dortoirs,
   Egrenant les bonnes semailles,
   En inclinant ta chaste taille
   Sur les sujets de tes devoirs.

   Ah! pour une âme trop tanguée,   70
   Tes baisers sont des potions
   Qui la laissent là, bien droguée,
   Et s'oubliant à te voir gaie,
   Accomplissant tes fonctions
   En point narquoise Déléguée.   75

LES COMMUNIANTES

Des ramiers
Familiers
Sous nos jupes palpitent!
Doux Çakya, venez vite
Les faire prisonniers!   80

LE FIGUIER

Défaillantes, les Etoiles que la lumière
Epuise, battent plus faiblement des paupières.

Le vert-luisant s'éteint à bout, l'Etre pâmé
Agonise à tâtons et se meurt à jamais.

Et l'Idéal égrène en ses mains fugitives   85
L'éternel chapelet des planètes plaintives.

Pauvres fous, vraiment pauvres fous!
Puis, quand on a fait la crapule,
On revient geindre au crépuscule,
Roulant son front dans les genoux   90
Des Saintes bouddhiques Nounous.

Complainte de cette bonne Lune

On entend les Etoiles :
   Dans l'giron
   Du Patron,
  On y danse, on y danse,
   Dans l'giron   5
   Du Patron,
  On y danse tous en rond.

—Là, voyons, mam'zell' la Lune,
Ne gardons pas ainsi rancune;
Entrez en danse, et vous aurez   10
Un collier de soleils dorés.

—Mon Dieu, c'est à vous bien honnête,
Pour une pauvre Cendrillon;
Mais, me suffit le médaillon
Que m'a donné ma sœur planète.   15

—Fi! votre Terre est un suppôt
De la Pensée! Entrez en fête;
Pour sûr, vous tournerez la tête
Aux astres les plus comme il faut.

—Merci, merci, je n'ai que ma mie,   20
Juste que je l'entends gémir!

—Vous vous trompez, c'est le soupir
Des universelles chimies!

—Mauvaises langues, taisez-vous!
Je dois veiller. Tas de traînées,   25
Allez courir vos guilledous!

—Va donc, rosière enfarinée!
Hé! Notre-Dame des gens soûls,
Des filous et des loups-garous!
Metteuse en rut des vieux matous!   30
    Coucou!

Exeunt les étoiles. Silence et Lune. On entend:

            Sous l'plafond
              Sans fond,
        On y danse, on y danse
            Sous l'plafond   35
              Sans fond,
        On y danse tous en rond.

Complainte des Pianos qu'on entend dans les Quartiers aisés

Menez l'âme que les Lettres ont bien nourrie,
Les pianos, les pianos, dans les quartiers aisés!
Premiers soirs, sans pardessus, chaste flânerie,
Aux complaintes des nerfs incompris ou brisés.

    Ces enfants, à quoi rêvent-elles,   5
    Dans les ennuis des ritournelles?

        —'Préaux des soirs,
        Christs des dortoirs!

    'Tu t'en vas et tu nous laisses,
    Tu nous laiss's et tu t'en vas,   10
    Défaire et refaire ses tresses,
    Broder d'éternels canevas.'

Jolie ou vague? triste ou sage? encore pure?
O jours, tout m'est égal? ou, monde, moi je veux?
Et si vierge, du moins, de la bonne blessure   15
Sachant quels gras couchants ont les plus blancs aveux?

    Mon Dieu, à quoi donc rêvent-elles?
    A des Roland, à des dentelles?

        —'Cœurs en prison,
        Lentes saisons!   20

    'Tu t'en vas et tu nous quittes,
    Tu nous quitt's et tu t'en vas!
    Couvents gris, chœurs de Sulamites,
    Sur nos seins nuls croisons nos bras.'

Fatales clés de l'être un beau jour apparues;   25
Psitt! aux hérédités en ponctuels ferments,
Dans le bal incessant de nos étranges rues;
Ah! pensionnats, théâtres, journaux, romans!

Allez, stériles ritournelles,
La vie est vraie et criminelle.   30

    —'Rideaux tirés,
    Peut-on entrer?

'Tu t'en vas et tu nous laisses,
Tu nous laiss's et tu t'en vas,
La source des frais rosiers baisse,   35
Vraiment! Et lui qui ne vient pas...'

Il viendra! Vous serez les pauvres cœurs en faute,
Fiancés au remords comme aux essais sans fond,
Et les suffisants cœurs cossus, n'ayant d'autre hôte
Qu'un train-train pavoisé d'estime et de chiffons.   40

    Mourir? peut-être brodent-elles,
    Pour un oncle à dot, des bretelles?

        —'Jamais! Jamais!
        Si tu savais!

'Tu t'en vas et tu nous quittes,   45
Tu nous quitt's et tu t'en vas,
Mais tu nous reviendras bien vite
Guérir mon beau mal, n'est-ce pas?'

Et c'est vrai! l'Idéal les fait divaguer toutes,
Vigne bohême, même en ces quartiers aisés.   50
La vie est là; le pur flacon des vives gouttes
Sera, *comme il convient*, d'eau propre baptisé.

    Aussi, bientôt, se joueront-elles
    De plus exactes ritournelles.

        '—Seul oreiller!   55
        Mur familier!

'Tu t'en vas et tu nous laisses,
Tu nous laiss's et tu t'en vas,
Que ne suis-je morte à la messe!
O mois, ô linges, ô repas!   60

Complainte de la bonne Défunte

Elle fuyait par l'avenue,
Je la suivais illuminé,
Ses yeux disaient: 'J'ai deviné
Hélas! que tu m'as reconnue!'   4

Je la suivis illuminé!
Yeux désolés, bouche ingénue,
Pourquoi l'avais-je reconnue,
Elle, loyal rêve mort-né?   8

Yeux trop mûrs, mais bouche ingénue;
Œillet blanc, d'azur trop veiné;
Oh! oui, rien qu'un rêve mort-né,
Car, défunte elle est devenue.   12

Gis, œillet, d'azur trop veiné,
La vie humaine continue
Sans toi, défunte devenue.
—Oh! je rentrerai sans dîner!   16

Vrai, je ne l'ai jamais connue.

Complainte de l'Orgue de Barbarie

Orgue, orgue de Barbarie,
Don Quichotte, Souffre-Douleur,
Vidasse, vidasse ton cœur,
Ma pauvre rosse endolorie.   4

    Hein, étés idiots,
    Octobres malades,
    Printemps, purges fades,
    Hivers tout vieillots?   8

—'Quel silence, dans la forêt d'automne,
Quand le soleil en son sang s'abandonne!'

    Gaz, haillons d'affiches,
    Feu les casinos,   12
    Cercueils des pianos,
    Ah! mortels postiches.

—'Déjà la nuit, qu'on surveille à peine
Le frou-frou de sa titubante traîne.'   16

    Romans pour les quais,
    Photos élégiaques,
    Escarpins, vieux claques,
    D'un coup de balai!'   20

—'Oh! j'ai peur, nous avons perdu la route;
Paul, ce bois est mal famé! chut, écoute...'

    Végétal fidèle,
    Eve aime toujours   24
    LUI! jamais pour
    Nous, jamais pour elle.

—'O ballets corrosifs! réel, le crime?
La lune me pardonnait dans les cimes.'   28

     Vêpres, Ostensoirs,
     Couchants! Sulamites
     De province aux rites
     Exilants des soirs!   32

—'Ils m'ont brûlée; et depuis, vagabonde
Au fond des bois frais, j'implore le monde.'

     Et les vents s'engueulent,
     Tout le long des nuits!   36
     Qu'est-c'que moi j'y puis,
     Qu'est-ce donc qu'ils veulent?

—'Je vais guérir, voyez la cicatrice,
Oh! je ne veux pas aller à l'hospice!'   40

     Des berceaux fienteux
     Aux bières de même,
     Bons couples sans gêne,
     Tournez deux à deux.   44

Orgue, Orgue de Barbarie!
Scie autant que Souffre-Douleur,
Vidasse, vidasse ton cœur,
Ma pauvre rosse endolorie.   48

Complainte d'un certain Dimanche

> Elle ne concevait pas qu'aimer fut l'ennemi d'aimer.
> SAINTE-BEUVE. *Volupté.*

L'homme n'est pas méchant, ni la femme éphémère.
Ah! fous dont au casino battent les talons,
Tout homme pleure un jour et toute femme est mère,
    Nous sommes tous filials, allons!
Mais quoi! les Destins ont des parti-pris si tristes,   5
Qui font que, les uns loin des autres, l'on s'exile,
Qu'on se traite à tort et à travers d'égoïstes,
Et qu'on s'use à trouver quelque unique Evangile.
Ah! jusqu'à ce que la nature soit bien bonne,
    Moi je veux vivre monotone.   10

Dans ce village en falaises, loin, vers les cloches,
Je redescends dévisagé par les enfants
Qui s'en vont faire bénir de tièdes brioches;
    Et rentré, mon sacré-cœur se fend!
Les moineaux des vieux toits pépient à ma fenêtre,   15
Ils me regardent dîner, sans faim, à la carte;
Des âmes d'amis morts les habitent peut-être?
Je leur jette du pain: comme blessés, ils partent!
Ah! jusqu'à ce que la nature soit bien bonne,
    Moi je veux vivre monotone.   20

Elle est partie hier. Suis-je pas triste d'elle?
Mais c'est vrai! Voilà donc le fond de mon chagrin!
Oh! ma vie est aux plis de ta jupe fidèle!
    Son mouchoir me flottait sur le Rhin...
Seul.—Le Couchant retient un moment son Quadrige   25
En rayons où le ballet des moucherons danse,
Puis, vers les toits fumants de la soupe, il s'afflige...
Et c'est le Soir, l'insaisissable confidence...

Ah! jusqu'à ce que la nature soit bien bonne,
    Faudra-t-il vivre monotone?   30

Que d'yeux, en éventail, en ogive, ou d'inceste,
Depuis que l'Etre espère, ont réclamé leurs droits!
O ciels, les yeux pourrissent-ils comme le reste?
    Oh! qu'il fait seul! oh! fait-il froid!
Oh! que d'après-midi d'automne à vivre encore!   35
Le Spleen, eunuque à froid, sur nos rêves se vautre!
Or, ne pouvant redevenir des madrépores,
O mes humains, consolons-nous les uns les autres.
Et jusqu'à ce que la nature soit bien bonne,
    Tâchons de vivre monotone.   40

Complainte d'un autre Dimanche

C'était un très-au vent d'octobre paysage,
Que découpe, aujourd'hui dimanche, la fenêtre,
Avec sa jalousie en travers, hors d'usage,
Où sèche, depuis quand! une paire de guêtres
Tachant de deux mals blancs ce glabre paysage.   5

Un couchant mal bâti suppurant du livide;
Le coin d'une buanderie aux tuiles sales;
En plein, le Val-de-Grâce, comme un qui préside;
Cinq arbres en proie à de mesquines rafales
Qui marbrent ce ciel crû de bandages livides.   10

Puis les squelettes des glycines aux ficelles,
En proie à des rafales encor plus mesquines!
O lendemains de noce! ô bribes de dentelles!
Montrent-elles assez la corde, ces glycines
Recroquevillant leur agonie aux ficelles!   15

Ah! qu'est-ce que je fais, ici, dans cette chambre!
Des vers. Et puis, après? ô sordide limace!
Quoi! la vie est unique, et toi, sous ce scaphandre,
Tu te racontes sans fin, et tu te ressasses!
Seras-tu donc toujours un qui garde la chambre?   20

Ce fut un bien au vent d'octobre paysage...

Complainte du Fœtus de Poète

Blasé dis-je! En avant,
Déchirer la nuit gluante des racines,
A travers maman, amour tout d'albumine,
Vers le plus clair! vers l'alme et riche étamine
    D'un soleil levant!   5

—Chacun son tour, il est temps que je m'émancipe,
Irradiant des Limbes mon inédit type!

    En avant!
Sauvé des steppes du mucus, à la nage
Têter soleil! et soûl de lait d'or, bavant,   10
Dodo à des seins dorloteurs des nuages,
    Voyageurs savants!

—A rêve que veux-tu, là-bas, je vivrai dupe
D'une âme en coup de vent dans la fraîcheur des jupes!

    En avant!   15
Dodo sur le lait caillé des bons nuages
Dans la main de Dieu, bleue, aux mille yeux vivants
Aux pays du vin viril faire naufrage!
    Courage,
    Là, là, je me dégage...   20

—Et je communierai, le front vers l'Orient,
Sous les espèces des baisers inconscients!

    En avant!
Cogne, glas des nuits! filtre, soleil solide!
Adieu, forêts d'aquarium qui, me couvant,   25
Avez mis ce levain dans ma chrysalide!
    Mais j'ai froid? En avant!
    Ah! maman...

Vous, Madame, allaitez le plus longtemps possible
Et du plus Seul de vous ce pauvre enfant-terrible.   30

Complainte des Pubertés difficiles

Un éléphant de Jade, oeil mi-clos souriant,
Méditait sous la riche éternelle pendule,
Bon bouddha d'exilé qui trouve ridicule
Qu'on pleure vers les Nils des couchants d'Orient,
  Quand bave notre crépuscule.   5

  Mais, sot Eden de Florian,
En un vase de Sèvre où de fins bergers fades
S'offrent des bouquets bleus et des moutons frisés,
Un oeillet expirait ses pubères baisers
Sous la trompe sans flair de l'éléphant de Jade. 10

  A ces bergers peints de pommade
Dans le lait, à ce couple impuissant d'opéra
Transi jusqu'au trépas en la pâte de Sèvres,
Un gros petit dieu Pan venu de Tanagra
Tendait ses bras tout inconscients et ses lèvres. 15

  Sourds aux vanités de Paris,
  Les lauriers fanés des tentures,
  Les mascarons d'or des lambris,
  Les bouquins aux pâles reliures
  Tournoyaient par la pièce obscure,   20
  Chantant, sans orgueil, sans mépris:
'Tout est frais dès qu'on veut comprendre la Nature.'

Mais lui, cabré devant ces soirs accoutumés,
Où montait la gaîté des enfants de son âge,
Seul au balcon, disait, les yeux brûlés de rages: 25
'J'ai du génie, enfin: nulle ne veut m'aimer!'

Complainte de la Fin des Journées

Vous qui passez, oyez donc un pauvre être,
Chassé des *Simples* qu'on peut reconnaître
Soignant, las, quelque œillet à leur fenêtre!
     Passants, hâtifs passants,
Oh! qui veut visiter les palais de mes sens?   5

       Maints ciboires
       De déboires,
       Un encor!

Ah! l'enfant qui vit de ce nom, poète!
Il se rêvait, seul, pansant Philoctète   10
Aux nuits de Lemnos; ou, loin, grêle ascète.
     Et des vers aux moineaux,
Par le lycée en vacances, sous les préaux!

       Offertoire,
       En mémoire   15
       D'un consort.

Mon Dieu, que tout fait signe de se taire!
Mon Dieu, qu'on est follement solitaire!
Où sont tes yeux, premier dieu de la Terre
      Qui ravala ce cri: 20
'Têtue Eternité! je m'en vais incompris...'?

       Pauvre histoire!
       Transitoire?
       Passe-port?

J'ai dit: mon Dieu. La terre est orpheline   25
Aux ciels, parmi les séminaires des Routines.
Va, suis quelque robe de mousseline…
        —Inconsciente Loi;
Faites que ce crachoir s'éloigne un peu de moi!

            Vomitoire   30
            De la Foire,
            C'est la mort.

Complainte de la Vigie aux Minuits polaires

Le Globe, vers l'aimant,
Chemine exactement,
Tinté de mers si bleues,
De cités tout en toits,   4
De réseaux de convois
Qui grignottent des lieues.

O ma côte en sanglots!
Pas loin de Saint-Malo,   8
Un bourg fumeux vivotte,
Qui tient sous son clocher,
Ou grince un coq perché,
L'Ex-Voto d'un pilote!   12

Aux cierges, au vitrail,
D'un autel en corail,
Une jeune Madone
Tend, d'un air ébaubi,   16
Un beau cœur de rubis
Qui se meurt et rayonne!

Un gros cœur tout en sang,
Un bon cœur ruisselant,   20
Qui, du soir à l'aurore,
Et de l'aurore au soir,
Se meurt, de ne pouvoir
Saigner, ah! saigner plus encore!   24

Complainte de la Lune en Province

Ah! la belle pleine Lune,
Grosse comme une fortune!

La retraite sonne au loin,
Un passant, monsieur l'adjoint;   4

Un clavecin joue en face,
Un chat traverse la place:

La province qui s'endort!
Plaquant un dernier accord,   8

Le piano clôt sa fenêtre.
Quelle heure peut-il bien être?

Calme Lune, quel exil!
Faut-il dire: ainsi soit-il?   12

Lune, ô dilettante Lune,
A tous les climats commune,

Tu vis hier le Missouri,
Et les remparts de Paris,   16

Les fiords bleus de la Norwège,
Les pôles, les mers, que sais-je?

Lune heureuse! ainsi tu vois,
A cette heure, le convoi   20

De son voyage de noce!
Ils sont partis pour l'Ecosse.

Quel panneau, si, cet hiver,
Elle eût pris au mot mes vers!   24

Lune, vagabonde Lune,
Faisons cause et mœurs communes?

O riches nuits! je me meurs,
La province dans le cœur!   28

Et la lune a, bonne vieille,
Du coton dans les oreilles.

Complainte des Printemps

Permettez, ô sirène,
Voici que votre haleine
Embaume la verveine;
C'est l'printemps qui s'amène! 4

—Ce système, en effet, ramène le printemps,
Avec son impudent cortège d'excitants.

Otez donc ces mitaines;
Et n'ayez, inhumaine, 8
Que mes soupirs pour traîne:
Ous'qu'il y a de la gêne...

—Ah! yeux bleus méditant sur l'ennui de leur art!
Et vous, jeunes divins, aux soirs crus de hasard! 12

Du géant à la naine,
Vois, tout bon sire entraîne
Quelque contemporaine,
Prendre l'air, par hygiène... 16

—Mais vous saignez ainsi pour l'amour de l'exil!
Pour l'amour de l'Amour! D'ailleurs, ainsi soit-il...

T'ai-je fait de la peine?
Oh! viens vers les fontaines 20
Où tournent les phalènes
Des Nuits Elyséennes!

—Pimbèche aux yeux vaincus, bellâtre aux beaux jarrets
Donnez votre fumier à la fleur du Regret. 24

Voilà que son haleine
N'embaum' plus la verveine!
Drôle de phénomène...
Hein, à l'année prochaine?   28

—Vierges d'hier, ce soir traîneuses de fœtus,
A genoux! voici l'heure où se plaint l'Angelus.

Nous n'irons plus aux bois,
Les pins sont éternels,   32
Les cors ont des appels!...

Neiges des pâles mois,
Vous serez mon missel!
—Jusqu'au jour de dégel.   36

Complainte de l'Automne monotone

Automne, automne, adieux de l'Adieu!
La tisane bout, noyant mon feu;
Le vent s'époumonne
A reverdir la bûche où mon grand cœur tisonne.
Est-il de vrais yeux?   5
Nulle ne songe à m'aimer un peu.

Milieux aptères,
Ou sans divans;
Regards levants,
Deuils solitaires   10
Vers des Sectaires!

Le vent, la pluie, oh! le vent, la pluie!
Antigone, écartez mon rideau;
Cet ex-ciel tout suie,
Fond-il *decrescendo, statu quo, crescendo*?   15
Le vent qui s'ennuie,
Retourne-t-il bien les parapluies?

Amours, gibiers!
Aux jours de givre,
Rêver sans livre,   20
Dans les terriers
Chauds de fumiers!

Plages, chemins de fer, ciels, bois morts,
Bateaux croupis dans les feuilles d'or,
Le quart aux étoiles,   25
Paris grasseyant par chic aux prises de voiles:
De trop poignants cors
M'ont hallalisé ces chers décors.

Meurtres, alertes,
Rêves ingrats!   30
En croix, les bras;
Roses ouvertes,
Divines pertes!

Le soleil mort, tout nous abandonne.
Il se crut incompris. Qu'il est loin!   35
    Vent pauvre, aiguillonne
Ces convois de martyrs se prenant à témoins!
    La terre, si bonne,
    S'en va, pour sûr, passer cet automne.

Nuits sous-marines!   40
Pourpres forêts,
Torrents de frais,
Bancs en gésines,
Tout s'illumine!

—Allons, fumons une pipette de tabac,   45
En feuilletant un de ces si vieux almanachs,

En rêvant de la petite qui unirait
Aux charmes de l'œillet ceux du chardonneret.

Complainte de l'Ange incurable

Je t'expire mes Cœurs bien barbouillés de cendres;
Vent esquinté de toux des paysages tendres!

Où vont les gants d'avril, et les rames d'antan?
L'âme des hérons fous sanglote sur l'étang.   4

       Et vous, tendres
       D'antan?

Le hoche-queue pépie aux écluses gelées;
L'amante va, fouettée aux plaintes des allées.   8

Sais-tu bien, folle pure, où sans châle tu vas?
—Passant oublié des yeux gais, j'aime là-bas...

       —En allées
       Là-bas!   12

Le long des marbriers (Encore un beau commerce!)
Patauge aux défoncés un convoi, sous l'averse.

Un trou, qu'asperge un prêtre âgé qui se morfond,
Bâille à ce libéré de l'être; et voici qu'on   16

       Le déverse
       Au fond.

Les moulins décharnés, ailes hier allègres,
Vois, s'en font les grands bras du haut des coteaux maigres!   20

Ci-gît n'importe qui. Seras-tu différent,
Diaphane d'amour, ô Chevalier-Errant?

Claque, ô maigre
Errant! 24

Hurler avec les loups, aimer nos demoiselles,
Serrer ces mains sauçant dans de vagues vaisselles!

Mon pauvre vieux, il le faut pourtant! et puis, va,
Vivre est encor le meilleur parti ici-bas. 28

Non! vaisselles
D'ici-bas!

Au-delà plus sûr que la Vérité! des ailes
D'Hostie ivre et ravie aux cités sensuelles! 32

Quoi? Ni Dieu, ni l'art, ni ma Sœur Fidèle; mais
Des ailes! par le blanc suffoquant! à jamais,

Ah! des ailes
A jamais! 36

—Tant il est vrai que la saison dite d'automne
N'est aux cœurs mal fichus rien moins que folichonne.

Complainte des Nostalgies préhistoriques

La nuit bruine sur les villes.
Mal repu des gains machinals,
On dîne; et gonflé d'idéal,
Chacun sirote son idylle,
      Ou furtive, ou facile.   5

Echos des grands soirs primitifs!
Couchants aux flambantes usines,
Rude paix des sols en gésine,
Cri jailli là-bas d'un massif,
      Voluptés à vif!   10

Dégringolant une vallée,
Heurter, dans des coquelicots,
Une enfant bestiale et brûlée,
Qui suce, en blaguant les échos,
      De juteux abricots.   15

Livrer aux langueurs des soirées
Sa toison où du cristal luit,
Pourlécher ses lèvres sucrées,
Nous barbouiller le corps de fruits
      Et lutter comme essui!   20

Un moment, béer, sans rien dire,
Inquiets d'une étoile là-haut;
Puis, sans but, bien gentils satyres,
Nous prendre aux premiers sanglots
      Fraternels des crapauds.   25

Et, nous délèvrant de l'extase,
Oh! devant la lune en son plein,
Là-bas, comme un bloc de topaze,
Fous, nous renverser sur les reins,
   Riant, battant des mains!   30

La nuit bruine sur les villes:
Se raser le masque, s'orner
D'un frac deuil, avec art dîner,
Puis, parmi des vierges débiles,
   Prendre un air imbécile.   35

Autre Complainte de l'Orgue de Barbarie

Prolixe et monocorde,
Le vent dolent des nuits
Rabâche ses ennuis,
Veut se pendre à la corde   4
   Des puits! et puis?
   Miséricorde!

—Voyons, qu'est-ce que je veux?
Rien. Je suis-t-il malhûreux!   8

Oui, les phares aspergent
Les côtes en sanglots,
Mais les volets sont clos
Aux veilleuses des vierges,   12
   Orgue au galop,
   Larmes des cierges!

—Après? qu'est-ce qu'on y peut?
—Rien. Je suis-t-il malhûreux!   16

Vous, fidèle madone,
Laissez! Ai-je assisté,
Moi, votre puberté?
O jours où Dieu tâtonne,   20
   Passants d'été,
   Pistes d'automne!

—Eh bien! aimerais-tu mieux...
—Rien. Je suis-t-il malhûreux!   24

Cultes, Littératures,
Yeux chauds, lointains ou gais,
Infinis au rabais,
Tout train-train, rien qui dure,   28
    Oh! à jamais
    Des créatures!

—Ah! ça qu'est-ce que je veux?
—Rien. Je suis-t-il malhûreux!   32

Bagnes des pauvres bêtes,
Tarifs d'alleluias,
Mortes aux camélias,
Oh! lendemain de fête   36
    Et paria,
    Vrai, des planètes!

—Enfin! quels sont donc tes vœux?
—Nuls. Je suis-t-il malhûreux!   40

La nuit monte, armistice
Des cités, des labours.
Mais il n'est pas, bon sourd,
En ton digne exercice,   44
    De raison pour
    Que tu finisses?

—Bien sûr. C'est ce que je veux.
Ah! Je suis-t-il malhûreux!   48

Complainte du pauvre Chevalier-Errant

Jupes des quinze ans, aurores de femmes,
Qui veut, enfin, des palais de mon âme?
Perrons d'œillets blancs, escaliers de flamme,
    Labyrinthes alanguis,   4
      Edens qui
Sonneront, sous vos pas reconnus, des airs reconquis.

Instincts-levants souriant par les fentes,
Méditations un doigt à la tempe,   8
Souvenirs clignotant comme des lampes,
    Et, battant les corridors,
      Vains essors,
Les Dilettantismes chargés de colliers de remords.   12

Oui, sans bruit, vous écarterez mes branches,
Et verrez comme, à votre mine franche,
Viendront à vous mes biches les plus blanches,
    Mes ibis sacrés, mes chats,   16
      Et, rachats!
Ma Vipère de Lettres aux bien effaçables crachats.

Puis, frêle mise au monde! ô Toute Fine,
O ma Tout-universelle orpheline,   20
Au fond de chapelles de mousseline
    Pâle, ou jonquille à pois noirs,
      Dans les soirs,
Feu-d'artificeront envers vous mes sens encensoirs!   24

Nous organiserons de ces parties!
Mes caresses, naïvement serties,
Mourront, de ta gorge aux vierges hosties,
    Aux amandes de tes seins!   28
      O tocsins,
Des cœurs dans le roulis des empilements de coussins.

Tu t'abandonnes au Bon, moi j'abdique;
Nous nous comblons de nos deux Esthétiques;   32
Tu condimentes mes piments mystiques,
   J'assaisonne tes saisons;
     Nous blasons,
A force d'étapes sur nos collines, l'Horizon!   36

Puis j'ai des tas d'éternelles histoires,
O mers, ô volières de ma Mémoire!
Sans compter les passes évocatoires!
   Et quand tu t'endormiras,   40
     Dans les draps
D'un somme, je t'éventerai de lointains opéras.

Orage en deux cœurs, ou jets d'eau des siestes,
Tout sera Bien, contre ou selon ton geste,   44
Afin qu'à peine un prétexte te reste
   De froncer tes chers sourcils.
     Ce souci:
'Ah! suis-je née, infiniment, pour vivre par ici?'   48

—Mais j'ai beau parader, toutes s'en fichent!
Et je repars avec ma folle affiche,
Boniment incompris, piteux *sandwiche*:
   Au Bon Chevalier-Errant,   52
     Restaurant,
Hôtel meublé, Cabinets de lecture, prix courants.

Complainte des Formalités nuptiales

LUI

Allons, vous prendrez froid.

ELLE

Non; je suis un peu lasse.
Je voudrais écouter toujours ce cor de chasse!

LUI

Dis, veux-tu te vêtir de mon Être éperdu?

ELLE

Tu le sais; mais il fait si pur à la fenêtre...   5

LUI

Ah! tes yeux m'ont trahi l'Idéal à connaître;
Et je le veux, de tout l'univers de mon être!
     Dis, veux-tu?

ELLE

Devant cet univers, aussi, je me veux femme;
C'est pourquoi tu le sais. Mais quoi! ne m'as-tu pas   10
Prise toute déjà? par tes yeux, sans combats!
A la messe, au moment du grand Alleluia,
     N'as-tu pas eu mon âme?

LUI

Oui; mais l'Unique Loi veut que notre serment
Soit baptisé des roses de ta croix nouvelle;   15
Tes yeux se font mortels, mais ton destin m'appelle,
Car il sait que, pour naître aux moissons mutuelles,
Je dois te caresser bien singulièrement:

Vous verrez mon palais! vous verrez quelle vie!
J'ai de gros lexicons et des photographies,   20

    De l'eau, des fruits, maints tabacs,
    Moi, plus naïf qu'hypocondre,
    Vibrant de tact à me fondre,
    Trempé dans les célibats.

    Bon et grand comme les bêtes,   25
    Pointilleux mais emballé,
    Inconscient mais esthète,
    Oh! veux-tu nous en aller
    Vers les pôles dont vous êtes?

Vous verrez mes voiliers! vous verrez mes jongleurs!   30
Vous soignerez les fleurs de mon *bateau de fleurs*.

Vous verrez qu'il y en a plus que je n'en étale,
Et quels violets gros deuil sont ma couleur locale,

Et que mes yeux sont ces vases d'Election
Des Danaïdes où sans fin nous puiserions!   35

    Des prairies adorables,
    Loin des mufles des gens;
    Et, sous les ciels changeants,
    Maints hamacs incassables!

      Dans les jardins   40
      De nos instincts

Allons cueillir
De quoi guérir...

Cuirassés des calus de mainte expérience,
Ne mettant qu'en mes yeux leurs lettres de créance,   45
Les orgues de mes sens se feront vos martyrs
Vers des cieux sans échos étoilés à mourir!

ELLE

Tu le sais; mais tout est si décevant! ces choses
Me poignent, après tout, d'un infaillible émoi!
Raconte-moi ta vie, ou bien étourdis-moi.   50
Car je me sens obscure, et, je ne sais pourquoi,
Je me compare aux fleurs injustement écloses...

LUI

Tu verras, c'est un rêve. Et tu t'éveilleras
Guérie enfin du mal de pousser solitaire.
Puis, ma fine convalescente du Mystère,   55
On vous soignera bien, nuit et jour, seuls sur terre.
        Tu verras?

ELLE

Tu le sais. Ah!—si tu savais! car tu m'as prise!
Bien au-delà! avec tes yeux, qui me suffisent.
Oui, tes yeux francs seront désormais mon église.   60
        Avec nos regards seulement,
        Alors, scellons notre serment?

LUI

Allons, endormez-vous, mortelle fiancée.
Là, dans mes bras loyaux, sur mon grand cœur bercée,
Suffoquez aux parfums de l'unique pensée   65
Que la vie est sincère et m'a fait le plus fort,

ELLE

Tiens, on n'entend plus ce cor; vous savez, ce cor...

LUI

L'Ange des Loyautés l'a baisée aux deux tempes;
Elle dort maintenant dans l'angle de ma lampe.
      O Nuit, 70
    Fais-toi lointaine
    Avec ta traîne
      Qui bruit!

    O défaillance universelle!
Mon unique va naître aux moissons mutuelles! 75
    Pour les fortes roses de l'amour
      Elle va perdre, lys pubère,
      Ses nuances si solitaires,
        Pour être, à son tour,
        Dame d'atour 80
        De Maïa!

    Alleluia!

Complainte des Blackboulés

'Ni vous, ni votre art, monsieur.' C'était un dimanche,
    Vous savez où.
    A vos genoux,
Je suffoquai, suintant de longues larmes blanches.   4

L'orchestre du jardin jouait ce *'si tu m'aimes'*
    Que vous savez;
    Et je m'en vais
Depuis, et pour toujours, m'exilant sur ce thème.   8

Et toujours, ce refus si monstrueux m'effraie
    Et me confond
    Pour vous au fond,
Si Regard-Incarné! si moi-même! si vraie!   12

Bien.—Maintenant, voici ce que je vous souhaite,
    Puisque, après tout,
    En ce soir d'août,
Vous avez craché vers l'Art, par dessus ma tête.   16

Vieille et chauve à vingt ans, sois prise pour une autre,
    Et sans raison,
    Mise en prison,
Très loin, et qu'un geôlier, sur toi, des ans, se vautre.   20

Puis, passe à Charenton, parmi de vagues folles,
    Avec Paris
    Là-bas, fleuri,
Ah! rêve trop beau! Paris où je me console.   24

Et demande à manger, et qu'alors on confonde!
    Qu'on croie à ton
    Refus! et qu'on
Te nourisse, horreur! horreur! horreur! à la sonde.   28

La sonde t'entre par le nez, Dieu vous bénisse!
    A bas, les mains!
    Et le bon vin,
Le lait, les œufs te gavent par cet orifice.   32

Et qu'après bien des ans de cette facétie,
    Un interne (aux
    Regards loyaux!)
Se trompe de conduit! et verse, et t'asphyxie.   36

Et voilà ce que moi, guéri, je vous souhaite,
    Cœur rose, pour
    Avoir un jour
Craché sur l'Art! l'Art pur! sans compter le poète.   40

Complainte des Consolations

Quia voluit consolari.

Ses yeux ne me voient pas, son corps serait jaloux;
Elle m'a dit: 'monsieur...' en m'enterrant d'un geste;
Elle est Tout, l'univers moderne et le céleste.
Soit! draguons donc Paris, et ravitaillons-nous,
    Tant bien que mal, du reste. 5

Les Landes sans espoir de ses regards brûlés,
Semblaient parfois des paons prêts à mettre à la voile...
Sans chercher à me consoler vers les étoiles,
Ah! Je trouverai bien deux yeux aussi sans clés,
    Au Louvre, en quelque toile! 10

Oh! qu'incultes, ses airs, rêvant dans la prison
D'un *cant* sur le qui-vive au travers de nos hontes!...
Mais, en m'appliquant bien, moi dont la foi démonte
Les jours, les ciels, les nuits, dans les quatre saisons
    Je trouverai mon compte. 15

Sa bouche! à moi, ce pli pudiquement martyr
Où s'aigrissent des nostalgies de nostalgies!
Eh bien, j'irai parfois, très sincère vigie,
Du haut de Notre-Dame aider l'aube, au sortir,
    De passable orgies. 20

Mais, Tout va la reprendre!—Alors Tout m'en absout.
Mais, Elle est ton bonheur!—Non! je suis trop immense
Trop chose. Comment donc! mais ma seule présence
Ici-bas, vraie à s'y mirer, est l'air de Tout:
    De la Femme au Silence! 25

Complainte des bons Ménages

L'Art sans poitrine m'a trop longtemps bercé dupe.
Si ses labours sont fiers, que ses blés décevants!
Tiens, laisse-moi bêler tout aux plis de ta jupe
    Qui fleure le couvent. 4

Le Génie avec moi, serf, a fait des manières;
Toi, jupe, fais frou-frou, sans t'inquiéter pourquoi,
Sois l'œillet bleu de ciel de l'unique théière,
    Sois toi-même, à part moi. 8

Je veux être pendu, si tu n'es pas discrète
Et *comme il faut*, vraiment! Et d'ailleurs tu m'es tout.
Tiens, j'aimerais les plissés de ta colerette
    Sans en venir à bout. 12

Mais l'Art, c'est l'Inconnu! qu'on y dorme et s'y vautre.
On peut ne pas l'avoir constamment sur les bras!
Eh bien, ménage au vent! Soyons Lui, Elle et l'Autre.
    Et puis, n'insistons pas. 16

Complainte de lord Pierrot

Au clair de la lune,
Mon ami Pierrot,
Filons, en costume,
Présider là-haut!
Ma cervelle est morte,   5
Que le Christ l'emporte!
Béons à la Lune,
La bouche en zéro.

Inconscient, descendez en nous par réflexes;
Brouillez les cartes, les dictionnaires, les sexes.   10

Tournons d'abord sur nous-même, comme un fakir!
(Agiter le pauvre être, avant de s'en servir.)

J'ai le cœur chaste et vrai comme une bonne lampe;
Oui, je suis en taille douce, comme une estampe.

Vénus, énorme comme le Régent,   15
Déjà se pâme à l'horizon des grèves;
Et c'est l'heure, ô gens nés casés, bonnes gens,
De s'étourdir en longs trilles de rêves!
Corybanthe, aux quatre vents tous les draps!
Disloque tes pudeurs, à bas les lignes!   20
En costume blanc, je ferai le cygne,
Après nous le Déluge, ô ma Léda!
Jusqu'à ce que tournent tes yeux vitreux,
Que tu grelottes en rires affreux,
Hop! enlevons sur les horizons fades   25
Les menuets de nos pantalonnades!
     Tiens! l'Univers
     Est à l'envers...
—Tout cela vous honore,
Lord Pierrot, mais encore?   30

—Ah! qu'une, d'elle-même, un beau soir sût venir,
Ne voyant que boire à mes lèvres, ou mourir!

Je serais, savez-vous, la plus noble conquête
Que femme, au plus ravi du Rêve, eût jamais faite!

    D'ici là, qu'il me soit permis   35
    De vivre de vieux compromis!

    Où commence, où finit l'humaine
    Ou la divine dignité?

    Jonglons avec les entités,
    Pierrot s'agite et Tout le mène!   40
    Laissez faire, laissez passer;
    Laissez passer, et laissez faire:
    Le semblable, c'est le contraire,

    Et l'univers c'est pas assez!
    Et je me sens, ayant pour cible   45
    Adopté la vie impossible,
    De moins en moins localisé!

    —Tout cela vous honore,
    Lord Pierrot, mais encore?

    —Il faisait, ah! si chaud si sec.   50
    Voici qu'il pleut, qu'il pleut, bergères!
    Les pauvres Vénus bocagères
    Ont la roupie à leur nez grec!

    —Oh! de moins en moins drôle;
    Pierrot sait mal son rôle?   55

—J'ai le cœur triste comme un lampion forain...
Bah! j'irai passer la nuit dans le premier train;

    Sûr d'aller, ma vie entière,
    Malheureux comme les pierres. (*Bis*).

Autre Complainte de lord Pierrot

Celle qui doit me mettre au courant de la Femme!
Nous lui dirons d'abord, de mon air le moins froid:
'La somme des angles d'un triangle, chère âme,
    'Est égale à deux droits.'   4

Et si ce cri lui part: 'Dieu de Dieu que je t'aime!'
—'Dieu reconnaîtra les siens.' Ou piquée au vif:
—'Mes claviers ont du cœur, tu seras mon seul thème.'
    Moi: 'Tout est relatif.'   8

De tous ses yeux, alors! se sentant trop banale:
'Ah! tu ne m'aimes pas; tant d'autres sont jaloux!'
Et moi, d'un œil qui vers l'Inconscient s'emballe:
    'Merci, pas mal; et vous?'   12

—'Jouons au plus fidèle!'—'A quoi bon, ô Nature!
'Autant à qui perd gagne!' Alors, autre couplet:
—'Ah! tu te lasseras le premier, j'en suis sûre...'
    —'Après vous, s'il vous plaît.'   16

Enfin, si, par un soir, elle meurt dans mes livres,
Douce; feignant de n'en pas croire encor mes yeux,
J'aurai un: 'Ah! ça, mais, nous avions De Quoi vivre!
    'C'était donc sérieux?'   20

Complainte sur certains Ennuis

Un couchant des Cosmogonies!
Ah! que la Vie est quotidienne...
Et, du plus vrai qu'on se souvienne,
Comme on fut piètre et sans génie...   4

On voudrait s'avouer des choses,
Dont on s'étonnerait en route,
Qui feraient une fois pour toutes!
Qu'on s'entendrait à travers poses.   8

On voudrait saigner le Silence,
Secouer l'exil des causeries;
Et non! ces dames sont aigries
Par des questions de préséance.   12

Elles boudent là, l'air capable.
Et, sous le ciel, plus d'un s'explique,
Par quel gâchis suresthétiques
Ces êtres-là sont adorables.   16

Justement, une nous appelle,
Pour l'aider à chercher sa bague,
Perdue (où dans ce terrain vague?)
Un souvenir D'AMOUR, dit-elle!   20

Ces êtres-là sont adorables!

Complainte des Noces de Pierrot

Où te flatter pour boire dieu,
Ma provisoire corybante?
Je sauce mon âme en tes yeux,
Je ceins ta beauté pénitente,   4
Où donc vis-tu? Moi si pieux,
    Que tu m'es lente, lente!

Tes cils m'insinuent: c'en est trop;
Et leurs calices vont se clore,   8
Sans me jeter leur dernier mot,
Et refouler mes métaphores,
De leur petit air comme il faut?
    Isis, levez le store!   12

Car cette fois, c'est pour de bon;
Trop d'avrils, quittant la partie
Devant des charmes moribonds,
J'ai bâclé notre eucharistie   16
Sous les trépieds où ne répond
    Qu'une aveugle Pythie!

Ton tabernacle est dévasté?
Sois sage, distraite égoïste!   20
D'ailleurs, suppôt d'éternité,
Le spleen de tout ce qui s'existe
Veut qu'en ce blanc matin d'été,
    Je sois ton exorciste!   24

Ainsi, fustigeons ces airs plats
Et ces dolentes pantomimes
Couvrant d'avance du vieux glas
Mes tocsins à l'hostie ultime!   28
Ah! tu me comprends n'est-ce pas,
    Toi, ma moins pauvre rime?

Introïbo, voici l'Epoux !
Hallali ! songe au pôle, aspire ;   32
Je t'achèterai des bijoux,
Garde moi ton *ut* de martyre...
Quoi ! bébé bercé, c'est donc tout ?
    Tu n'as plus rien à dire ?   36

—Mon dieu, mon dieu ! je n'ai rien eu,
J'en suis encore aux poncifs thèmes !
Son teint me redevient connu,
Et, sur son front tout au baptême,   40
Aube déjà l'air ingénu !
L'air vrai ! l'air non mortel quand même !

    Ce qui fait que je l'aime,

    Et qu'elle est même, vraiment,   44
      La chapelle rose
      Où parfois j'expose
      Le Saint-Sacrement
    De mon humeur du moment.   48

Complainte du Vent qui s'ennuie la nuit

Ta fleur se fane, ô fiancée?
Oh! gardes-en encore un peu
La corolle qu'a compulsée
Un soir d'ennui trop studieux!   4
Le vent des toits qui pleure et rage,
Dans ses assauts et ses remords,
Sied au nostalgique naufrage
Où m'a jeté ta Toison-d'Or.   8

        Le vent assiège,
            Dans sa tour,
        Le sortilège
            De l'Amour;   12
        Et, pris au piège,
        Le sacrilège
        Geint sans retour.

Ainsi, mon Idéal sans bride   16
T'ubiquitait de ses sanglots,
O calice loyal mais vide
Qui jouais à me rester clos!
Ainsi dans la nuit investie,   20
Sur tes pétales décevants,
L'Ange fileur d'eucharisties
S'afflige tout le long du vent.

        Le vent assiège,   24
            Dans sa tour,
        Le sortilège
            De l'Amour,
        Et, pris au piège,   28
            Le sacrilège,
        Geint sans retour.

O toi qu'un remords fait si morte,
Qu'il m'est incurable, en tes yeux,   32
D'écouter se morfondre aux portes
Le vent aux étendards de cieux!
Rideaux verts de notre hypogée,
Marbre banal du lavabo,   36
Votre hébétude ravagée
Est le miroir de mon tombeau.

    O vent, allège
      Ton discours   40
    Des vains cortèges
      De l'humour;
    Je rentre au piège,
    Peut-être y vais-je,   44
    Tuer l'Amour!

Complainte du pauvre Corps humain

L'Homme et sa compagne sont serfs
De corps, tourbillonnants cloaques
Aux mailles de harpes de nerfs
Serves de tout et que détraque
Un fier répertoire d'attaques.   5

    Voyez l'homme, voyez!
    Si ça n'fait pas pitié!

Propre et correct en ses ressorts,
S'assaisonnant de modes vaines,
Il s'admire, ce brave corps,   10
Et s'endimanche pour sa peine,
Quand il a bien sué la semaine.

    Et sa compagne! allons,
    Ma bell'; nous nous valons.

Faudrait le voir, touchant et nu   15
Dans un décor d'oiseaux, de roses;
Ses tics réflexes d'ingénu,
Ses plis pris de mondaines poses;
Bref, sur beau fond vert, sa chlorose,

    Voyez l'Homme, voyez!   20
    Si ça n'fait pas pitié!

Les Vertus et les Voluptés
Détraquant d'un rien sa machine,
Il ne vit que pour disputer
Ce domaine à rentes divines   25
Aux lois de mort qui le taquinent.

Et sa compagne! allons,
Ma bell', nous nous valons.

Il se soutient de mets pleins d'art,
Se drogue, se tond, se parfume,   30
Se truffe tant, qu'il meurt trop tard;
Et la cuisine se résume
En mille infections posthumes.

    Oh! ce couple, voyez!
    Non, ça fait trop pitié.   35

Mais ce microbe subversif
Ne compte pas pour la Substance,
Dont les déluges corrosifs
Renoient vite pour l'Innocence
Ces fols germes de conscience.   40

    Nature est sans pitié
    Pour son petit dernier.

Complainte du Roi de Thulé

Il était un roi de Thulé,
    Immaculé,
Qui, loin des jupes et des choses,
Pleurait sur la métempsychose   4
    Des lys en roses,
    Et quel palais!

Ses fleurs dormant, il s'en allait,
    Traînant des clés,   8
Broder aux seuls yeux des étoiles,
Sur une tour, un certain Voile
    De vive toile,
    Aux nuits de lait!   12

Quand le voile fut bien ourlé,
    Loin de Thulé,
Il rama fort sur les mers grises,
Vers le soleil qui s'agonise,   16
    Féerique Eglise!
    Il ululait:

'Soleil-crevant, encore un jour,
Vous avez tendu votre phare   20
Aux holocaustes vivipares,
Du culte qu'ils nomment l'Amour.

'Et comme, devant la nuit fauve,
Vous vous sentez défaillir,   24
D'un dernier flot d'un sang martyr
Vous lavez le seuil de l'Alcôve!

'Soleil! Soleil! moi je descends
Vers vos navrants palais polaires,　　　　28
Dorloter dans ce Saint-Suaire
　　　Votre cœur bien en sang,
　　　En le berçant!'

Il dit, et, le Voile étendu,　　　　32
　　　Tout éperdu,
Vers les coraux et les naufrages,
Le roi raillé des doux corsages,
　　　Beau comme un Mage　　　　36
　　　Est descendu!

Braves amants! aux nuits de lait,
　　　Tournez vos clés!
Une ombre, d'amour pur transie,　　　　40
Viendrait vous gémir cette scie:
'Il était un roi de Thulé
　　　Immaculé...'

Complainte du Soir des Comices Agricoles

Deux royaux cors de chasse ont encore un duo
      Aux échos,
Quelques fusées reniflent s'étouffer là-haut!

      Allez, allez, gens de la noce,
      Qu'on s'en donne une fière bosse!   5

Et comme le jour naît, que bientôt il faudra,
      A deux bras,
Peiner, se recrotter dans les labours ingrats,

      Allez, allez, gens que vous êtes,
      C'est pas tous les jours jour de fête!   10

Ce violon incompris pleure au pays natal,
      Loin du bal,
Et le piston risque un appel vers l'Idéal...

      Mais le flageolet les rappelle,
      Et allez donc, mâl's et femelles!   15

Un couple erre parmi les rêves des grillons,
      Aux sillons;
La fille écoute en tourmentant son médaillon.

      Laissez, laissez, ô cors de chasse,
      Puisque c'est le sort de la race.   20

Les beaux cors se sont morts; mais cependant qu'au loin,
      Dans les foins,
Crêvent deux rêves niais, sans maire et sans adjoint.

      Pintez, dansez, gens de la Terre,
      Tout est un triste et vieux Mystère.   25

—Ah! le Premier que prit ce besoin insensé
    De danser
Sur ce monde enfantin dans l'Inconnu lancé!

    O Terre, ô terre, ô race humaine,
    Vous me faites bien de la peine.   30

Complainte des Cloches

Dimanche, à Liège.

Bin bam, bin bam,
Les cloches, les cloches,
Chansons en l'air, pauvres reproches!
Bin bam, bin bam,
Les cloches en Brabant!　　　　5

Petits et gros, clochers en fête,
De l'hôpital à l'Evêché,
Dans ce bon ciel endimanché,
Se carillonnent, et s'entêtent,
A tue-tête! à tue-tête!　　　　10

Bons vitraux, saignez impuissants
Aux allégresses hosannahlles
Des orgues lâchant leurs pédales,
Les tuyaux bouchés par l'encens!
Car il descend! il descend!　　　　15

Voici les lentes oriflammes
Où flottent la Vierge et les Saints!
Les cloches, leur battant des mains,
S'étourdissent en jeunes gammes
Hymniclames! hymniclames!　　　　20

Va, Globe aux studieux pourchas,
Où Dieu à peine encor s'épèle!
Bondis, Jérusalem nouvelle,
Vers les nuits grosses de rachats,
Où les lys! ne filent pas!　　　　25

Edens mûrs, Unique Bohême!
Nous, les beaux anges effrénés;
Elles, des Regards incarnés,
Pouvant nous chanter, sans blasphème:
    Que je t'aime! pour moi-même!   30

Oui, les cloches viennent de loin!
Oui, oui, l'Idéal les fit fondre
Pour rendre les gens hypocondres,
Vêtus de noir, tendant le poing
    Vers un Témoin! Un Témoin!   35

Ah! cœur-battant, cogne à tue-tête
Vers ce ciel niais endimanché!
Clame, à jaillir de ton clocher,
Et nous retombe à jamais BÊTE.
    Quelle fête! quelle fête!   40

    Bin bam, bin bam,
    Les cloches! les cloches!
Chansons en l'air, pauvres reproches!
    Bin bam, bin bam,
    Les cloches en Brabant![1]   45

    [1] Et ailleurs.

Complainte des grands Pins dans une Villa abandonnée

A Bade

Tout hier, le soleil a boudé dans ses brumes,
Le vent jusqu'au matin n'a pas décoléré,
Mais, nous point des coteaux là-bas, un œil sacré
Qui va vous bousculer ces paquets de bitume !   4

    —Ah ! vous m'avez trop, trop vanné,
    Bals de diamants, hanches roses ;
    Et, bien sûr, je n'étais pas né
        Pour ces choses.   8

—Le vent jusqu'au matin n'a pas décoléré.
Oh ! ces quintes de toux d'un chaos bien posthume,

    —Prés et bois vendus ! Que de gens,
    Qui me tenaient mes gants, serviles,   12
    A cette heure, de mes argents,
        Font des piles !

—Délayant en ciels bas ces paquets de bitume
Qui grimpaient talonnés de noirs Misérérés !   16

    —Elles, coudes nus dans les fruits,
    Riant, changeant de doigts leurs bagues ;
    Comme nos plages et nos nuits
        Leur sont vagues !   20

—Oh ! ces quintes de toux d'un chaos bien posthume !
Chantons comme Memnon, le soleil a filtré,

—Et moi, je suis dans ce lit cru
De chambre d'hôtel, fade chambre,   24
Seul, battu dans les vents bourrus
    De novembre.

—Qui, consolant des vents les noirs Misérérés,
Des nuages en fuite éponge au loin l'écume.   28

    —Berthe aux sages yeux de lilas,
    Qui priais Dieu que je revinsse,
    Que fais-tu, mariée là-bas,
        En province?
                    32

—Memnons, ventriloquons! le cher astre a filtré
Et le voilà qui tout authentique s'exhume!

    —Oh! quel vent! adieu tout sommeil;
    Mon Dieu, que je suis bien malade!   36
    Oh! notre croisée au soleil
        Bon, à Bade.

—Il rompt ses digues! vers les grands labours qui fument!
Saint Sacrement! et *Labarum* des *Nox irae*!   40

    —Et bientôt, seul, je m'en irai,
    A Montmartre, en cinquième classe,
    Loin de père et mère, enterrés
        En Alsace.
                    44

Complainte sur certains Temps déplacés

Le couchant de sang est taché
Comme un tablier de boucher;
Oh! qui veut aussi m'écorcher!

—Maintenant c'est comme une rade!   4
Ça vous fait le cœur tout nomade,
À cingler vers mille Lusiades!

Passez, ô nuptials appels,
Vers les comptoirs, les Archipels   8
Où l'on mastique le bétel!

Je n'aurai jamais d'aventures;
Qu'il est petit, dans la Nature,
Le chemin d'fer Paris-Ceinture!   12

—V'là le fontainier! il siffle l'air
(Connu) du bon roi Dagobert;
Oh! ces matins d'avril en mer!

—Le vent galope ventre à terre,   16
En vain voudrait-on le fair'taire!
Ah! nom de Dieu quelle misère!

—Le Soleil est mirobolant
Comme un poitrail de chambellan,   20
J'en demeure les bras ballants;

Mais jugez si ça m'importune,
Je rêvais en plein de lagunes
De Venise au clair de la lune!   24

—Vrai! la vie est pour les badauds;
Quand on a du dieu sous la peau,
On cuve ça sans dire mot.

L'obélisque quadrangulaire, 28
De mon spleen monte; j'y digère,
En stylite, ce gros Mystère.

Complainte des Condoléances au Soleil

Décidément, bien don Quichotte et pas peu sale,
Ta Police, ô Soleil! malgré tes grands Levers,
Et tes couchants des beaux Sept-Glaives abreuvés,
Rosaces en sang d'une aveugle Cathédrale!   4

Sans trève, aux spleens d'amour sonner des hallalis!
Car, depuis que, majeur, ton fils calcule et pose,
Labarum des glaciers! fais-tu donc autre chose
Que chasser devant toi des dupes de leurs lits?   8

Certe, dès qu'aux rideaux aubadent tes fanfares,
Ces piteux d'infini, clignant de gluants deuils,
Rhabillent leurs tombeaux, en se cachant de l'œil
Qui cautérise les citernes les plus rares!   12

Mais tu ne te dis pas que, là-bas, bon Soleil,
L'autre moitié n'attendait que ta défaillance,
Et déjà se remet à ses expériences,
Alléguant quoi? la nuit, l'usage, le sommeil...   16

Or, à notre guichet, tu n'es pas mort encore,
Pour aller fustiger de rayons ces mortels,
Que nos bateaux sans fleurs rerâlent vers leurs ciels
D'où pleurent des remparts brodés contre l'aurore!   20

Alcôve des Danaïdes, triste astre!—Et puis,
Ces jours où, tes fureurs ayant fait les nuages,
Tu vas sans pouvoir les percer, blême de rage
De savoir seul et tout à ses aises l'Ennui!   24

Entre nous donc, bien don Quichotte, et pas moins sale,
Ta Police, ô Soleil, malgré tes grands Levers,
Et tes couchants des beaux Sept-Glaives abreuvés,
Rosaces en sang d'une aveugle Cathédrale!   28

Complainte de l'Oubli des Morts

Mesdames et Messieurs,
Vous dont la mère est morte,
C'est le bon fossoyeux
Qui gratte à votre porte.   4

    Les morts
    C'est sous terre;
    Ça n'en sort
      Guère.   8

Vous fumez dans vos bocks,
Vous soldez quelque idylle,
Là bas chante le coq,
Pauvres morts hors des villes!   12

Grand-papa se penchait,
Là, le doigt sur la tempe,
Sœur faisait du crochet,
Mère montait la lampe.   16

    Les morts
    C'est discret,
    Ça dort
    Trop au frais.   20

Vous avez bien dîné,
Comment va cette affaire?
Ah! les petits mort-nés
Ne se dorlotent guère!   24

Notez, d'un trait égal,
Au livre de la caisse,
Entre deux frais de bal:
Entretien tombe et messe.   28

C'est gai,
Cette vie;
Hein, ma mie,
O gué?   32

Mesdames et Messieurs,
Vous dont la sœur est morte,
Ouvrez au fossoyeux
Qui claque à votre porte;   36

Si vous n'avez pitié,
Il viendra (sans rancune)
Vous tirer par les pieds,
Une nuit de grand'lune!   40

Importun
Vent qui rage!
Les défunts?
Ça voyage...   44

Complainte du pauvre jeune Homme

Sur l'air populaire:
'Quand le bonhomm' revint du bois.'

Quand ce jeune homm' rentra chez lui,
Quand ce jeune homm' rentra chez lui;
Il prit à deux mains son vieux crâne,
Qui de science était un puits!
   Crâne,   5
  Riche crâne,
Entends-tu la Folie qui plane?
Et qui demande le cordon,
Digue dondaine, digue dondaine,
Et qui demande le cordon,   10
Digue dondaine, digue dondon!

Quand ce jeune homm' rentra chez lui,
Quand ce jeune homm' rentra chez lui,
Il entendit de tristes gammes,
Qu'un piano pleurait dans la nuit!   15
   Gammes,
  Vieilles gammes,
Ensemble, enfants, nous vous cherchâmes!
Son mari m'a fermé sa maison,
Digue dondaine, digue dondaine,   20
Son mari m'a fermé sa maison,
Digue dondaine, digue dondon!

Quand ce jeune homm' rentra chez lui,
Quand ce jeune homm' rentra chez lui;
Il mit le nez dans sa belle âme,   25
Où fermentaient des tas d'ennuis!
   Ame,
  Ma belle âme,
Leur huile est trop sal' pour ta flamme!

Puis, nuit partout! lors, à quoi bon?   30
Digue dondaine, digue dondaine,
Puis, nuit partout! lors, à quoi bon?
Digue dondaine, digue dondon!

Quand ce jeune homm' rentra chez lui,
Quand ce jeune homm' rentra chez lui;   35
Il vit que sa charmante femme,
Avait déménagé sans lui!
      Dame,
       Notre-Dame,
Je n'aurai pas un mot de blâme!   40
Mais t'aurais pu m'laisser l'charbon[1]
Digue dondaine, digue dondaine,
Mais t'aurais pu m'laisser l'charbon,
Digue dondaine, digue dondon.

Lors, ce jeune homme aux tels ennuis,   45
Lors, ce jeune homme aux tels ennuis;
Alla décrocher une lame,
Qu'on lui avait fait cadeau avec l'étui!
      Lame,
       Fine lame,   50
Soyez plus droite que la femme!
Et vous, mon Dieu, pardon! pardon!
Digue dondaine, digue dondaine,
Et vous, mon Dieu, pardon! pardon!
Digue dondaine, digue dondon!   55

Quand les croq'morts vinrent chez lui,
Quand les croq'morts vinrent chez lui;
Ils virent qu' c'était un' belle âme,
Comme on n'en fait plus aujourd'hui!
      Ame,   60
       Dors, belle âme!
Quand on est mort c'est pour de bon,
Digue dondaine, digue dondaine,
Quand on est mort c'est pour de bon,
Digue dondaine, digue dondon!   65

[1] Pour s'asphyxier.

Complainte de l'Epoux outragé

Sur l'air populaire:
'Qu'allais-tu faire à la fontaine?'

—Qu'alliez-vous faire à la Mad'leine,
    Corbleu, ma moitié,
Qu'alliez-vous faire à la Mad'leine?

—J'allais prier pour qu'un fils nous vienne,   4
    Mon Dieu, mon ami;
J'allais prier pour qu'un fils nous vienne.

—Vous vous teniez dans un coin, debout,
    Corbleu, ma moitié!   8
Vous vous teniez dans un coin debout.

—Pas d'chaise économis' trois sous,
    Mon Dieu, mon ami;
Pas d'chaise économis' trois sous.   12

—D'un officer, j'ai vu la tournure,
    Corbleu, ma moitié!
D'un officier, j'ai vu la tournure.

—C'était ce Christ grandeur nature,   16
    Mon Dieu, mon ami;
C'était ce Christ grandeur nature.

—Les Christs n'ont pas la croix d'honneur,
    Corbleu, ma moitié!   20
Les Christs n'ont pas la croix d'honneur.

—C'était la plaie du Calvaire, au cœur,
    Mon Dieu, mon ami;
C'était la plaie du Calvaire au cœur.   24

—Les Christs n'ont qu'au flanc seul la plaie,
    Corbleu, ma moitié!
Les Christs n'ont qu'au flanc seul la plaie!

—C'était une goutte envolée,   28
    Mon Dieu, mon ami;
C'était une goutte envolée.

—Aux Crucifix on n'parl' jamais,
    Corbleu, ma moitié!   32
Aux Crucifix on n'parl' jamais?

—C'était du trop d'amour qu' j'avais,
    Mon Dieu, mon ami,
C'était du trop d'amour qu' j'avais!   36

—Et moi j'te brûl'rai la cervelle,
    Corbleu, ma moitié,
Et moi j'te brûl'rai la cervelle!

Lui, il aura mon âme immortelle,   40
    Mon Dieu, mon ami,
Lui, il aura mon âme immortelle!

Complainte-Variations sur le mot 'Falot, Falotte'

Falot, falotte!
Sous l'aigre averse qui clapote,
Un chien aboie aux feux-follets,
Et puis se noie, taïaut, taïaut!   4
La Lune, voyant ces ballets,
   Rit à Pierrot!
Falot! falot!

Falot, Falotte!   8
Un train perdu, dans la nuit, stoppe
Par les avalanches bloqué;
Il siffle au loin! et les petiots
Croient ouïr les méchants hoquets   12
   D'un grand crapaud!
Falot, falot!

Falot, falotte!
La danse du bateau-pilote,   16
Sous l'œil d'or du phare, en péril!
Et sur les *steamers*, les galops
Des vents filtrant leurs longs exils
   Par les hublots!   20
Falot, falot!

Falot, falotte!
La petite vieille qui trotte,
Par les bois aux temps pluvieux,   24
Cassée en deux sous le fagot
Qui réchauffera de son mieux
   Son vieux fricot!
Falot, falot!   28
Falot, falotte!

Sous sa lanterne qui tremblotte,
Le fermier dans son potager
S'en vient cueillir des escargots,   32
Et c'est une étoile au berger
   Rêvant là haut!
   Falot, falot!

   Falot, falotte!   36
Le lumignon au vent toussotte,
Dans son cornet de gras papier;
Mais le passant en son pal'tot
O mandarines des Janviers,   40
   File au galop!
   Falot, falot!

   Falot, falotte!
Un chiffonnier va sous sa hotte;   44
Un réverbère près d'un mur
Où se cogne un vague soulaud,
Qui l'embrasse comme un pur,
   Avec des mots!   48
   Falot, falot!

   Falot, falotte!
Et c'est ma belle âme en ribotte,
Qui se sirote et se fait mal,   52
Et fait avec ses grands sanglots,
Sur les beaux lacs de l'Idéal
   Des ronds dans l'eau!
   Falot, falot!   56

Complainte du Temps et de sa Commère l'Espace

Je tends mes poignets universels dont aucun
N'est le droit ou le gauche, et l'Espace, dans un
Va-et-vient giratoire, y détrame les toiles
D'azur pleines de cocons à fœtus d'Etoiles.   4
Et nous nous blasons tant, je ne sais où, les deux
Indissolubles nuits aux orgues vaniteux
De nos pores à Soleils, où toute cellule
Chante : Moi ! Moi ! puis s'éparpille, ridicule !   8

Elle est l'infini sans fin, je deviens le temps
Infaillible. C'est pourquoi nous nous perdons tant.
Où sommes-nous ? Pourquoi ? Pour que Dieu s'accomplisse ?
Mais l'Eternité n'y a pas suffi ! Calice   12
Inconscient, où tout cœur crevé se résout,
Extrais-nous donc alors de ce néant trop tout !
Que tu fisses de nous seulement une flamme,
Un vrai sanglot mortel, la moindre goutte d'âme !   16

Mais nous bâillons de toute la force de nos
Touts, sûrs de la surdité des humains échos.
Que ne suis-je indivisible ! Et toi, douce Espace,
Où sont les steppes de tes seins, que j'y rêvasse ?   20
Quand t'ai-je fécondée ? Oh ! ce dut
Etre un spasme intéressant ! Mais quel fut mon but ?
Je t'ai, tu m'as. Mais où ? Partant, toujours. Extase
Sur laquelle, quand on est le Temps, on se blase.   24

Or, voilà des spleens infinis que je suis en
Voyage vers ta bouche, et pas plus à présent
Que toujours, je ne sens la fleur triomphatrice
Qui flotte, m'as-tu dit, au seuil de ta matrice.   28
Abstraites amours ! quel infini mitoyen
Tourne entre nos deux Touts ? Sommes nous deux ? ou bien,
(Tais-toi si tu ne peux me prouver à outrance,
Illico, le fondement de la connaissance,   32

Et, par ce chant: Pensée, Objet, Identité!
Souffler le Doute, songe d'un siècle d'été.)
Suis-je à jamais un solitaire Hermaphrodite,
Comme le Ver Solitaire, ô ma Sulamite?   36
Ma complainte n'a pas eu de commencement,
Que je sache, et n'aura nulle fin; autrement,
Je serais l'anachronisme absolu. Pullule
Donc, azur possédé du mètre et du pendule!   40

O Source du Possible, alimente à jamais
Des pollens des soleils d'exil, et de l'engrais
Des chaotiques hécatombes, l'automate
Universel où pas une loi ne se hâte.   44
Nuls à tout, sauf aux rares mystiques éclairs
Des Elus, nous restons les deux miroirs d'éther
Réfléchissant, jusqu'à la mort de ces Mystères,
Leurs Nuits que l'Amour distrait de fleurs éphémères.   48

Grande Complainte de la Ville de Paris

PROSE BLANCHE

Bonne gens qui m'écoutes, c'est Paris, Charenton compris.
Maison fondée en...à louer. Médailles à toutes les expositions
et des mentions. Bail immortel. Chantiers en gros et en
détail de bonheurs sur mesure. Fournisseurs brevetés d'un
tas de majestés. Maison recommandée. Prévient la chute   5
des cheveux. En loteries! Envoie en province. Pas de morte-
saison. Abonnements. Dépôt, sans garantie de l'humanité,
des ennuis les plus comme il faut et d'occasion. Facilités de
paiement, mais de l'argent. De l'argent, bonne gens!

Et ça se ravitaille, import et export, par vingt gares et   10
douanes. Que tristes, sous la pluie, les trains de marchandise!
A vous, dieux, chasublerie, ameublements d'église, dragées
pour baptêmes, le culte est au troisième, clientèle ineffable!
Amour, à toi, des maisons d'or aux hospices dont les langes
et loques feront le papier des billets doux à monogrammes,   15
trousseaux et layettes, seules eaux alcalines reconstituantes,
ô chlorose! bijoux de sérail, falbalas, tramways, miroirs de
poches, romances! Et à l'antipode, qu'y fait-on? Ça travaille,
pour que Paris se ravitaille...

D'ailleurs, des moindres pavés, monte le Lotus Tact. En   20
bataille rangée, les deux sexes, toilettés à la mode des
passants, mangeant dans le ruolz! Aux commis, des Nio-
bides; des faunesses aux Christs. Et sous les futaies seig-
neuriales des jardins très-publics, martyrs niaisant et vestales
minaudières faisant d'un clin d'œil l'article pour l'Idéal et   25
Cie (Maison vague, là-haut), mais d'elles-mêmes absentes,
pour sûr. Ah! l'Homme est un singulier monsieur; et elle, sa
voix de fausset, quel front désert! D'ailleurs avec du tact...

Mais l'inextirpable élite, d'où? pour où? Maisons de
blanc: pompes voluptiales; maisons de deuil: spleenuosités,   30
rancœurs à la carte. Et les banlieues adoptives, humus
teigneux, haridelles paissant bris de vaisselles, tessons,

semelles, de profil sur l'horizon des remparts. Et la pluie!
trois torchons à une claire-voie de mansarde. Un chien
aboie à un ballon là-haut. Et des coins claustrals, cloches   35
exilescentes des *dies iræmissibles*. Couchants d'aquarelliste
distinguée, ou de lapidaire en liquidation. Génie au prix de
fabrique, et ces jeunes gens s'entraînent en auto-litanies et
formules vaines, par vaines cigarettes. Que les vingt-quatre
heures vont vite à la discrète élite!...   40

    Mais les cris publics reprennent. Avis important!
l'Amortissable a fléchi, ferme le Panama. Enchères, experts.
Avances sur titres cotés ou non cotés, achats de nu-propriétés,
de viagers, d'usufruit; avances sur successions ouvertes et
autres; indicateurs, annuaires, étrennes. Voyages circulaires   45
à prix réduits. Madame Ludovic prédit l'avenir de 2 à 4.
Jouets *Au Paradis des enfants* et accessoires pour cotillons aux
grandes personnes. Grand choix de principes à l'épreuve.
Encore des cris! Seul dépôt! soupers de centième! Machines
cylindriques Marinoni! Tout garanti, tout pour rien! Ah!   50
la rapidité de la vie aussi seul dépôt...

    Des mois, les ans, calendriers d'occasion. Et l'automne
s'engrandeuille au bois de Boulogne, l'hiver gèle les fricots
des pauvres aux assiettes sans fleurs peintes. Mai purge, la
canicule aux brises frivoles des plages fane les toilettes   55
coûteuses. Puis, comme nous existons dans l'existence où
l'on paie comptant, s'amènent ces messieurs courtois des
Pompes Funèbres, autopsies et convois salués sous la vieille
Monotopaze du soleil. Et l'histoire va toujours dressant,
raturant ses Tables criblées de piteux *idem*, — ô Bilan, va   60
quelconque! ô Bilan, va quelconque...

Complainte des Mounis du Mont-Martre

Dire que, sans filtrer d'un divin Cœur,
Un air divin, et qui veut que tout s'aime,
   S'in-Pan-filtre, et sème
Ces vols d'oasis folles de blasphèmes
Vivant pour toucher quelque part un Cœur...   5

    Un tic-tac froid rit en nos poches,
    Chronomètres, réveils, coucous;
    Faut remonter ces beaux joujoux,
    Œufs à heures, mouches du coche,
    Là-haut s'éparpillant en cloches...   10

        Voici le soir,
        Grince, musique
        Hypertrophique
        Des remontoirs!

Dire que Tout est un Très-Sourd Mystère;   15
Et que le Temps, qu'on ne sait où saisir,
    Oui, pour l'avertir!
Sarcle à jamais les bons soleils martyrs,
O laps sans digues des nuits du Mystère!...

    Allez, coucous, réveils, pendules;   20
    Escadrons d'insectes d'acier,
    En un concert bien familier,
    Jouez sans fin des mandibules,
    L'Homme a besoin qu'on le stimule!

        Sûrs, chaque soir,   25
        De la musique,
        Hypertrophique
        Des remontoirs!

Moucherons, valseurs d'un soir de soleil,
Vous, tout comme nous, nerfs de la nature,   30
    Vous n'avez point cure
De ce que peut être cette aventure:
Les mondes penseurs s'errant au Soleil!

    Triturant bien l'heure en secondes,
En trois mil six-cents coups de dents,   35
De nos parts au gâteau du Temps
Ne faites qu'un hachis immonde
Devant lequel on se morfonde!

    Sûrs, chaque soir,
    De la musique   40
    Hypertrophique
    Des remontoirs!

Où le trouver, ce Temps, pour lui tout dire,
Lui mettre le nez dans son Œuvre, un peu!   45
    Et cesser ce jeu!
C'est vrai, la Métaphysique de Dieu
Et ses amours sont infinis!—mais, dire…

    Ah! plus d'heure? fleurir sans âge?
Voir les tableaux lents des Saisons   50
Régir l'écran des horizons,
Comme autant de belles images
D'un même Aujourd'hui qui voyage?

    Voici le soir!
    Grince, musique,   55
    Hypertrophique
    Des remontoirs!

Complainte-Litanies de mon Sacré-Cœur

Promethée et Vautour, châtiment et blasphème,
Mon Cœur, cancer sans cœur, se grignotte lui-même.

Mon Cœur est une urne où j'ai mis certains défunts,
Oh! chut, refrains de leurs berceaux! et vous, parfums...   4

Mon Cœur est un lexique où cent littératures
Se lardent sans répit de divines ratures.

Mon Cœur est un désert altéré, bien que soûl
De ce vin revomi, l'universel dégoût.   8

Mon Cœur est un Néron, enfant gâté d'Asie,
Qui d'empires de rêve en vain se rassasie.

Mon Cœur est un noyé vidé d'âme et d'essors,
Qu'étreint la pieuvre Spleen en ses ventouses d'or.   12

C'est un feu d'artifice hélas! qu'avant la fète,
A noyé sans retour l'averse qui s'embête.

Mon Cœur est le terrestre Histoire-Corbillard,
Que traînent au néant l'instinct et le hasard.   16

Mon Cœur est une horloge oubliée à demeure,
Qui, me sachant défunt, s'obstine à sonner l'heure!

Mon aimée était là, toute à me consoler;
Je l'ai trop fait souffrir, ça ne peut plus aller.   20

Mon Cœur, plongé au Styx de nos arts danaïdes,
Présente à tout baiser une armure de vide.

Et toujours, mon Cœur, ayant ainsi déclamé,
En revient à sa complainte: Aimer, être aimé!   24

Complainte des Débats mélancoliques et littéraires

On peut encore aimer, mais confier toute son âme
est un bonheur qu'on ne retrouvera plus.
CORINNE OU L'ITALIE.

Le long d'un ciel crépusculâtre,
Une cloche angéluse en paix
L'air exilescent et marâtre
Qui ne pardonnera jamais.   4

Paissant des débris de vaisselle,
Là-bas, au talus des remparts,
Se profile une haridelle
Convalescente; il se fait tard.   8

Qui m'aima jamais? Je m'entête
Sur ce refrain bien impuissant,
Sans songer que je suis bien bête
De me faire du mauvais sang.   12

Je possède un propre physique,
Un cœur d'enfant bien élevé,
Et pour un cerveau magnifique
Le mien n'est pas mal, vous savez!   16

Eh bien, ayant pleuré l'Histoire,
J'ai voulu vivre un brin heureux;
C'était trop demander, faut croire;
J'avais l'air de parler hébreux.   20

Ah! tiens, mon cœur, de grâce, laisse!
Lorsque j'y songe, en vérité,
J'en ai des sueurs de faiblesse,
A choir dans la malpropreté.   24

Le cœur me piaffe de génie
Eperdument pourtant, mon Dieu!
Et si quelqu'une veut ma vie,
Moi je ne demande pas mieux! 28

Eh va, pauvre âme véhémente!
Plonge, être, en leurs Jourdains blasés,
Deux frictions de vie courante
T'auront bien vite exorcisé. 32

Hélas, qui peut m'en répondre!
Tenez, peut-être savez-vous
Ce que c'est qu'une âme hypocondre?
J'en suis une dans les prix doux. 36

O Hélène, j'erre en ma chambre;
Et tandis que tu prends le thé,
Là-bas, dans l'or d'un fier septembre,
Je frissonne de tous mes membres, 40
En m'inquiétant de ta santé.

Tandis que, d'un autre côté...

Complainte d'une Convalescence en Mai

> Nous n'avons su toutes ces choses
> qu'après sa mort.
> VIE DE PASCAL par Mme Perier.

Convalescent au lit, ancré de courbatures,
Je me plains aux dessins bleus de ma couverture,

Las de reconstituer dans l'art du jour baissant
Cette dame d'en face auscultant les passants: 4

Si la Mort, de son van, avait chosé mon être,
En serait-elle moins, ce soir, à sa fenêtre?...

Oh! mort, tout mort! au plus jamais, au vrai néant
Des nuits où piaule en longs regrets le chant-huant!   8

Et voilà que mon Ame est tout hallucinée!
Puis s'abat, sans avoir fixé sa destinée.

Ah! que de soirs de mai pareils à celui-ci;
Que la vie est égale; et le cœur endurci!   12

Je me sens fou d'un tas de petites misères.
Mais maintenant, je sais ce qu'il me reste à faire.

Qui m'a jamais rêvé? Je voudrais le savoir!
Elles vous sourient avec âme, et puis bonsoir,   16

Ni vu ni connu. Et les voilà qui rebrodent
Le canevas ingrat de leur âme à la mode;

Fraîches à tous, et puis reprenant leur air sec
Pour les christs déclassés et autres gens suspects.   20

Et pourtant, le béni grand bol de lait de ferme
Que me serait un baiser sur sa bouche ferme!

Je ne veux accuser personne, bien qu'on eût
Pu, ce me semble, mon bon cœur étant connu...   24

N'est-ce pas; nous savons ce qu'il nous reste à faire,
O Cœur d'or pêtri d'aromates littéraires,

Et toi, cerveau confit dans l'alcool de l'Orgueil!
Et qu'il faut procéder d'abord par demi-deuils...   28

Primo: mes grandes angoisses métaphysiques
Sont passées à l'état de chagrins domestiques;

Deux ou trois spleens locaux—Ah! pitié, voyager
Du moins, pendant un an ou deux à l'étranger...   32

Plonger mon front dans l'eau des mers, aux matinées
Torrides, m'en aller à petites journées,

Compter les clochers, puis m'asseoir, ayant très chaud,
Aveuglé des maisons peintes au lait de chaux...   36

Dans les Indes du Rêve aux pacifiques Ganges,
Que j'en ai des comptoirs, des hamacs de rechange!

—Voici l'œuf à la coque et la lampe du soir.
Convalescence bien folle, comme on peut voir.   40

Complainte du Sage de Paris

Aimer, uniquement, ces jupes éphémères?
Autant dire aux soleils: fêtez vos centenaires.

Mais tu peux déguster, dans leurs jardins d'un jour,
Comme à cette dînette unique Tout concourt;   4

Déguster, en menant les rites réciproques,
Les trucs Inconscients dans leur œuf, à la coque.

Soit en pontifiant, avec toute ta foi
D'Exécuteur des hautes-œuvres de la Loi;   8

Soit en vivisectant ces claviers anonymes,
Pour l'art, sans espérer leur *ut* d'hostie ultime.

Car, crois pas que l'hostie où dort ton paradis
Sera d'une farine aux levains inédits.   12

Mais quoi, leurs yeux sont tout! et puis la nappe est mise,
Et l'Orgue juvénile à l'aveugle improvise.

Et, sans noce, voyage, curieux, colis,
Cancans, et fadeur d'hôpital du même lit,   16

Mais pour avoir des vitraux fiers à domicile,
Vivre à deux seuls est encor le moins imbécile.

Vois-la donc, comme d'ailleurs, et loyalement,
Les passants, les mots, les choses, les firmaments.   20

Vendange chez les arts enfantins; sois en fête
D'une fugue, d'un mot, d'un ton, d'un air de tête.

La science, outre qu'elle ne peut rien savoir,
Trouve, tels les ballons, l'Irrespirable Noir.   24

Ne force jamais tes pouvoirs de Créature,
Tout est écrit et vrai, rien n'est contre-nature.

Vivre et penser selon le Beau, le Bien, le Vrai?
O parfums, ô regards, ô fois! soit, j'essaierai;   28

Mais, tel Brennus avec son épée, et d'avance,
Suis-je pas dans l'un des plateaux de la balance?

Des casiers de bureau, le Beau, le Vrai, le Bien;
Rime et sois grand, la Loi reconnaîtra les siens.   32

Ah! demaillotte-toi, mon enfant, de ces langes
D'Occident! va faire une pleine eau dans le Gange.

La logique, la morale, c'est vite dit;
Mais! gisements d'instincts, virtuels paradis,   36

Nuit des hérédités et limbes des latences!
Actif? passif? ô pelouses des Défaillances,

Tamis de pores! Et les bas-fonds sous-marins,
Infini sans foyer, forêt vierge à tous crins!   40

Pour voir, jetez la sonde, ou plongez sous la cloche;
Oh! les velléités, les anguilles sous roche,

Les polypes sournois attendant l'hameçon,
Les vœux sans état-civil, ni chair, ni poisson!   44

Les guanos à Geysers, les astres en syncope,
Et les métaux qui font loucher nos spectroscopes!

Une capsule éclate, un monde de facteurs
En prurit, s'éparpille assiéger les hauteurs;   48

D'autres titubent sous les butins génitoires,
Ou font un feu d'enfer dans leurs laboratoires!

Allez! laissez passer, laissez faire; l'Amour
Reconnaîtra les siens: il est aveugle et sourd.   52

Car la vie innombrable va, vannant les germes
Aux concurrences des êtres sans droits, sans terme.

Vivottez et passez, à la grâce de Tout;
Et voilà la piété, l'amour et le bon goût.   56

L'Insconscient, c'est l'Eden-Levant que tout saigne;
Si la Terre ne veut sécher, qu'elle s'y baigne!

C'est la grande Nounou où nous nous aimerions
A la grâce des divines sélections.   60

C'est le Tout-Vrai, l'Omniversel Ombelliforme
Mancenilier, sous qui, mes bébés, faut qu'on dorme!

(Nos découvertes scientifiques étant
Ses feuilles mortes, qui tombent de temps en temps.)   64

Là, sur des oreillers d'étiquettes d'éthiques,
Lévite félin aux égaux ronrons lyriques,

Sans songer: 'Suis-je-moi? Tout est si compliqué!
'Où serais-je à présent, pour tel coche manqué?'   68

Sans colère, rire, ou pathos, d'une foi pâle,
Aux riches flirtations des pompes argutiales,

Mais sans rite emprunté, car c'est bien malséant,
Sirote chaque jour ta tasse de néant;   72

Lavé comme une hostie, en quelconques costumes
Blancs ou deuil, bref calice au vent qu'un rien parfume.

—'Mais, tout est un rire à la Justice! et d'où vient
Mon cœur, ah! mon sacré-cœur, s'il ne rime à rien?'   76

—Du calme et des fleurs. Peu t'importe de connaître
Ce que tu fus, dans l'à jamais, avant de naître?

Eh bien, que l'autre éternité qui, Très-Sans-Toi,
Grouillera, te laisse aussi pieusement froid.   80

Quant à *ta* mort, l'éclair aveugle en est en route
Qui saura te choser, va, sans que tu t'en doutes.

—'Il rit d'oiseaux, le pin dont *mon* cercueil viendra!'
—Mais *ton* cercueil sera *sa* mort! etc...   84

Allons, tu m'as compris. Va, que ta seule étude
Soit de vivre sans but, fou de mansuétude.

Complainte des Complaintes

Maintenant! pourquoi ces complaintes?
Gerbes d'ailleurs d'un défunt Moi
Où l'ivraie art mange la foi?
Sot tabernacle où je m'éreinte   4
A cultiver des roses peintes?
Pourtant ménage et sainte-table!
Ah! ces complaintes incurables,
     Pourquoi? pourquoi?   8

Puis, Gens à qui les fugues vraies
Que crie, au fond, ma riche voix
—N'est-ce pas, qu'on les sent parfois?—
Attoucheraient sous leurs ivraies   12
Les violettes d'une Foi,
Vous passerez, imperméables
A mes complaintes incurables?
     Pourquoi? pourquoi?   16

Chut! tout est bien, rien ne s'étonne.
Fleuris, ô Terre d'occasion,
Vers les mirages des Sions!
Et nous, sous l'Art qui nous bâtonne,   20
Sisyphes par persuasion,
Flûtant des christs les vaines fables,
Au cabestan de l'incurable
     POURQUOI!—Pourquoi?   24

Complainte-Epitaphe

La Femme,
Mon âme :
Ah! quels
Appels!   4

Pastels
Mortels,
Qu'on blâme
Mes gammes!   8

Un fou
S'avance,
Et danse.

Silence...   12
Lui, où?
Coucou.

COMMENTARIES

PREAMBLE

Les Complaintes is a very unequal volume of some fifty poems arranged in groups which are rather more different from each other than at first appears. Inevitably, critical commentary on them must be unequal too. The strength of the volume undoubtedly derives from the poems written during 1883 and 1884 and amongst these are poems like 'Complainte des Pianos qu'on entend dans les Quartiers aisés', 'Complainte d'un certain Dimanche', 'Complainte d'un autre Dimanche', 'Complainte du Roi de Thulé', 'Complainte des grands Pins dans une Villa abandonnée' and 'Complainte d'une Convalescence en Mai'—fine poems which are better than anything Laforgue wrote before 1886. A frank acceptance of the unevenness of the volume will at least leave space for an adequate introductory critique of these poems.

Two categories of weaker poem do not really merit the same degree of critical attention. In the first are those early poems which Laforgue might have been well advised to exclude, poems first written before the volume as a whole was conceived and before he began to use the word 'complainte'. The matter is discussed in some detail both in the Introduction and in Chapter II of the companion monograph, but for immediate critical purposes 'early' tends to mean rhetorical, inclining towards the verbose, contemporary with *Le Sanglot de la Terre*, imitative or derivative, 'Philosophical'. When Laforgue defended himself in correspondence with Paris friends for his desire to retain 'Préludes autobiographiques', written in 1880, he understandably did not draw attention to the fact that other poems, perhaps as many as ten, were also contemporary with the rejected *Le Sanglot de la Terre*. Some of these he re-wrote and included at the last moment to fill out the volume. Of course a reader will have to decide for himself whether the volume would have been better without these poems. Probably it would have been.

In the second category are poems whose effects are largely verbal. It was in 1883 that Laforgue wrote those of the 'Complaintes' that are based on or are analogous to street tunes and popular songs. Some of these, where the element of song is part of a more complex fabric, are amongst Laforgue's best poems. Others, where interest in word sounds predominates, are so limited to the verbal that extended discussion would be inappropriate. It is possibly incorrect to call these poems weak, since they at least give variety to the book and are in fact part of its originality. Brevity of comment on a poem in this category, therefore, does not mean dismissal but simply acceptance of the poem's limited purposes.

The inherent unevenness of the volume raises questions of critical strategy. Both the brilliant and the unexceptional poems tend to be allusive, cryptic, difficult and demand discussion. On the other hand, successful or unsuccessful, the poems draw heavily upon a central stock of image and metaphor, specifically the nihilistic or decadent formulations which Laforgue had derived initially from Schopenhauer and Hartmann. These formulations, or sets of ideas and attitudes, occur in poem after poem and the reader soon realizes that almost every imaginative experience, whatever its occasion, will be expressed in this language. These considerations, taken together, create difficulties for the commentator. To treat each poem equally would be to repeat the exegesis of this terminology of decadence, already sufficiently discussed in the Athlone Press monograph on Laforgue. That monograph apart, the serious student will have read or re-read Schopenhauer and Hartmann for himself. Or, if he has not, he will quickly become aware of repeated motifs, images, metaphors and will not look for an introductory discussion of them in each and every poem. Consequently, it needs to be said at the outset that the notes and commentaries which follow are arranged sequentially, more for the convenience perhaps of the reader who reads continuously from beginning to end than for the one who uses the notes because interested in single poems. This sequential arrangement is possible because the first few poems in the volume are early 'philosophical' poems with a high density of this decadent terminology that Laforgue made peculiarly his own. Once the reader realizes how Laforgue habitually sees things repeated explanations are unnecessary. This, at least, has been assumed.

Of course this thematic deployment of words and ideas from Hartmann and Schopenhauer is only one example of a repetitiveness of poetic idiom that does not need an equivalent repetitiveness of critical discussion. Another example would be the youthful Laforgue's retention of the vocabulary of lost faith. Instead of abandoning the language of the Church, which would have been consistent with his atheism, he retained it as psychological or emotional metaphor for the anguish of disbelief. This inversion suited his anti-bourgeois, iconoclastic purposes: to shock by distorting what normal people considered to be sacred obviously satisfied him, particularly in his early poems. In retrospect, however, it seems tedious, merely iconoclastic and overdone. Extended commentary simply is not needed for something so obvious. Another example might be Laforgue's fascination with the eye as a sexual image. In poem after poem, how people look at each other and how they notice the movement of each other's eyes is the metaphor either for their relationship or, more frequently, for their alienation, until the word: *yeux* becomes almost a code word for unfulfilled desire. To discuss this type of repeated motif on each occasion it occurs would be superfluous.

A similar question of critical strategy concerns Laforgue's vocabulary. It quickly becomes clear that there are two categories of difficulty. Sometimes a poem seems impenetrable simply because of the bizarre, or extravagant, or exotic language, because the words themselves simply as words are so unusual. Sometimes these words occur in passages which are syntactically or grammatically difficult. To distinguish sharply between these two poetic 'situations' is, of course, impossible except in a preamble of this kind, because it is a matter of critical judgement or discrimination to decide whether the effect of a certain passage comes from the exotic vocabulary in itself or from Laforgue's use of it. In a general way, however, there is more emphasis in these commentaries on the need to determine the internal poetic logic of poems which are structurally or syntactically obscure than on the defining of words that are unfamiliar. Laforgue said himself that he wished to achieve novelty at all cost and that one of the methods he adopted was to cull his dictionaries, especially his Littré. Often such words are arresting solely because their physical shape, their sound, their resonances are unfamiliar: this is why Laforgue is sometimes criticized for being too 'verbal'. At all events, the reader new to Laforgue must in this matter fend for himself. He, too, will need his Littré or equivalent dictionary, which in many instances will be a sufficient guide to passages which are brilliantly fabricated but which are not inherently obscure. This being the case, there will be no attempt to 'explain' or 'translate' unfamiliar words unless the context itself justifies or demands critical discussion.

Not only are words, motifs, metaphors, repeated throughout the volume, but so also are Laforgue's attitudes and preoccupations. His attitude to experience was instinctively, automatically negative; he was preoccupied with failure, lack of fulfilment, loneliness, misunderstanding. The implications or the meaning of his hostility to normal experience are discussed fairly extensively in Chapter IV of the companion monograph. Here, it is sufficient to say that Laforgue created whole sets or sequences of poems whose main effect derives from the ironic, bitter, cynical or merely frivolous disruption or inversion of normal meanings.

If these poems have their distinctive quality, arouse distinctive pleasures, it is because of their irony, their wit. Whether this wit is sufficient to hold in balance Laforgue's preoccupation with the fact, as it is treated here, of personal loneliness and sexual frustration is a critical question that arises, in only slightly different ways, in poem after poem. Most readers will feel that Laforgue is frequently perverse; that he, as the 'Ego' of his poem, desires love and yet is wilful in his denial of its significance; that he is sexually lonely and frustrated and yet remains stubborn in his unwillingness to accept the implications of his position; that he craves companionship and is therefore wrong-headed in dwelling so heavily on alienation, broken friendships, sexual inequalities and personal failure. On the other hand, Laforgue is not merely perverse. Loneliness, sexual deprivation, alienation, unhappiness and the deep depression that comes to a person impressed by the meaninglessness, as he sees it, of existence are all real enough, troublesome enough. Here again the reader will see that there is repetition, sometimes lightly ironical, sometimes bitter and self-pitying, in a variety of poems. It would be a waste of time and space to analyse repeatedly this complex of attitude and preoccupation that is so central to the volume as a whole. The emphasis of the commentaries will therefore not be on this type of explanation but on those features of particular poems which differentiate them imaginatively. Only if this procedure is adopted will there be the opportunity for genuine discussion of the more interestingly distinctive poems, some of which are brilliantly original.

Finally, the text. As mentioned in the Preface, the copy-text for the present edition is the first edition of 1885, reprinted unchanged except for the silent correction of blatantly obvious typographical errors. Because it is the policy of the Series to regard the first edition text as an important historical document whose features, good or bad, established at the time the poet's reputation, textual problems are only discussed in the critical commentaries which follow when they affect questions of interpretation. In other cases, the reader of the present edition will simply know that differences between the first edition text reproduced here and other available editions reflect various editors' attempts to tidy up the mess created if not caused by the first printer.

A PAUL BOURGET

The precise relationship between Laforgue and Paul Bourget is not clear. Certainly Laforgue looked up to him as an essentially modern writer and thinker, while Bourget felt sure enough about Laforgue's abilities to recommend him to the Empress Augusta. The link of friendship was a shared interest in poetry and a set of advanced cosmopolitan attitudes of the kind described in Bourget's *Essais de Psychologie Contemporaine*. Laforgue frequently admitted to Bourget's influence in his correspondence. As to the cosmopolitanism, it amounted to an appreciation that psychological rather than moral concerns would inform the art of the immediate future. For Bourget, these psychological concerns consisted of sets of fine perceptions of the kind later celebrated by Proust and described by Robert Louis Stevenson (in his letters on Bourget). For Laforgue they consisted of an uncomplicated acceptance of the primacy of sense perception, the actuality of which was more 'real' than any abstract thought or idealization. The reed pipe ('cha-lumeau') of this poet is therefore the nerve end.

By the time *Les Complaintes* appeared, the careers of Laforgue and Paul Bourget were already diverging. Bourget for a number of years devoted his best energies to the novel, a form which makes indifference to the world in which other people live virtually impossible. Laforgue was proceeding rapidly towards the greater imaginative freedom of his last poems. It seems probable, because of this divergence, that Bourget would not have been able to associate himself with Laforgue's self-portrait in this dedicatory poem. The 'brave bouddhiste' of l. 7 is the intellectual Buddhist from Schopenhauer, a figure not distinguished by religious mysticism but by an ascetic rejection of the world in which he lived, a symbol for the anti-bourgeois and for the indifference of an individual who observes, but is not involved in, the futility of human existence. The poet is enshrined in a temple reached through the open parkland of the esoteric. This esoteric world, securely remote from the everyday, is not green and fertile but white and infertile: the normal processes of existence are denied. The poet himself is a misfit ('albe' which relates to the root sense clear in the noun 'albinisme'), decaying or decadent ('oxydé' meaning almost literally 'eroded by life'), without purpose ('sans but'), and different (for 'pervers' does not mean per-verted but, in Darwinian terms, 'not part of the main stream'). The asceticism the poet attributes to himself in l. 13 is not moral but intellectual: the temple is the temple of a mind not concerned with the ordinary world. It was in this context that he called himself 'à jamais Innocent' in l. 4: the poet is innocent of involvement in the world and is more concerned with the metaphysical. From this remote vantage point, the dedication seems to say, *Les Complaintes* was written. Despite the respect expressed in the third stanza in the contrast between Bourget, 'ô pur poëte', and 'mes feuilleteurs du quai', Laforgue's more ordinary imaginative work, Bourget in all likelihood would have disapproved of this stance, of this almost aggressively Nihilistic description of a poet.

He certainly would not have approved of the vile pun in 'les cent pur-sang / De ses vingt ans', least of all when he came to realize that it anticipated the abuse of normal usage represented by the neologisms of later poems.

Laforgue was twenty-five when the poems were published: why then 'de ses vingt ans'? The matter is not important but perhaps this poem, as well as 'Préludes Autobiographiques', dates from 1880, before Laforgue went to Germany. In fact there are other poems in which Laforgue referred to his age and all of them must have been written before he went to Germany.

PRELUDES AUTOBIOGRAPHIQUES

Evidently Laforgue found himself under pressure from Charles Henry and Gustave Kahn to omit this poem, which they knew dated from 1880 and which in artistic terms has so little to do with *Les Complaintes*. 'Penses-tu comme le mathématicien du coin que je doive sacrifier cet *alléluia-préface* qui me semble à moi servir si passablement de toile de fond avec son air enfant et passé', Laforgue asked Kahn in February 1885. The volume would obviously be better without this clumsy poem, which shows that his preoccupation with his own development prevented him from thinking about the effect it would have on the volume. He knew that there was in fact a connection between his intellectual position in 1880 and the freely written 'Complaintes' of 1883. He wished, indulgently, to retain the poem as evidence of the fact that his new poems, however light-hearted or iconoclastic, had a serious basis. But a reader who enjoys the best of the poems will probably not care much about their intellectual origins or will perceive them easily without the promptings of the 'Préludes'.

Laforgue, though, was adamant. He returned to the matter in a letter written to Kahn a month later: 'Maintenant, sauf vos deux respects, je maintiendrai volontiers la pièce préface. Elle est faite avec des vers d'antan, elle est bruyante, et compatissable—elle est autobiographique. J'ai sacrifié un gros volume de vers philo. d'autrefois parce qu'ils étaient mauvais manifestement, mais enfin ce fut une étape et je tiens à dire (aux quelques [*sic*] à qui j'enverrai le volume), qu'avant d'être dilettante et pierrot j'ai séjourné dans le Cosmique.' Taken seriously, this statement would undermine the integrity of the volume since it calls in question the fundamental rationale of the more freely written poems. The poem itself, however, makes a completely serious response difficult. One is therefore left with the bare fact that Laforgue chose to surround or encase the 'Complaintes' written in 1883 and 1884 with earlier poems salvaged from the rejected *Le Sanglot de la Terre*.

In one sense, he obviously made a mistake. The poems in which the autobiographical element is denied or muted, whatever their value in more general terms, are simply more enjoyable than the early confessions and soul searchings written out in flat-footed alexandrines, as in this instance. On the other hand, a charitable reader will appreciate Laforgue's feelings about the chances of having freely written, fragmented, non-metrical poems accepted in 1885. He felt they had to be introduced and justified to a reading public unprepared for them. 'Préludes Autobiographiques' does this by reference to Hartmann's *Philosophie de l'Inconscient*.

The capitalized 'Tout' of the poem is that totality of a universe that exists and continues to exist irrespective of the life of the individual human being. Individuals are of no account. This particular individual walks through the streets of Paris at Christmas time, along the *quais* and past Notre-Dame, a derisory creature who is detached from Christian and indeed from the seasonal festivity, yet anxious for the consolations of the infinite. Why 'dérisoire' the reader must ask? Either life has meaning or it has not. If not, cries of anguish about man's predicament are also meaningless. And tedious. The adolescent yearning for absolutes is natural enough but phrases like 'dérisoire créature', 'des chagrins de la Terre' and 'Aux monstruosités sans but' are, for all that, extreme and sensational. The poet was struggling, he says ('ivre-mort de doute, / Je vivotais') but for what particular cause, for what special *angst*, the reader does not yet know. Is it the loneliness of the Nihilist? Or is it the more ordinary loneliness of someone who craves affection? This remains unresolved in Laforgue. In his autobiographical work, and this is confessedly an autobiographical poem, there lingers the suspicion that actual happiness, were it ever experienced, would soon overpower Laforgue's Nihilism: the 'Complaintes' of 1883 and 1884 are in a sense a demonstration of this, in that he was a happier person in the spring of 1883 when he wrote the lighter, artistically more accomplished poems. Yet the suspicion exists only on the level of speculation. The poet-figure in 'Préludes Autobiographiques' in fact confesses to an 'Etre ou Néant' type of loneliness, yearns for an understanding of the Unconscious that transcends the day-by-day, and is disappointed: 'Ni Témoin, ni spectacle!' From the tantalizing world of sense impression ('Lyres de nerfs...') one might as well revert to the condition of an unthinking, unreflective organism ('Redevenez plasma'), since the only vibrations (vibes?) one can feel insist on the ultimate disaster of existence. No solution to the problem of existence can be expected:

> Et que Jamais soit Tout, bien intrinsèquement,
> Très hermétiquement, primordialement.

A detailed exegesis of 'Préludes Autobiographiques' is impossible in the space available. At best one can point to those features of Laforgue's imaginative world which, whether in this poem or elsewhere, demonstrate what he meant by 'sojourning in the Cosmic'. Together they constitute a complex of ideas and emotions here serving as 'back drop' for the poems which follow. What are the salient elements in this? First, the river, the Seine along whose banks the poet walks, is 'Fleuve à reflets', not a symbol of something profound or mysterious but of the transitory and impenetrable. Absolute concepts, whether Christian or Atheist, do not endure. The world of the poet is the universe in which earth is only one of many stars—a star where whatever happens is meaningless and automatic: 'Et la création fonctionne têtue!' (l. 70). Thus the cathedral is 'anonyme'—it represents nothing of personal significance; the districts of the city are 'tannés'—worn, weathered, part of an immutable process; and the poet, separated from his fellow men ('bon mysogine'), lives more in the imaginative world of books than the real world of Paris, like a diver exploring the underwater world that in Laforgue, as in other writers, represents the unconscious—the psychological depths in which the mind exists when alienated from the physical surface world. These ideas, whether imaginative or 'philosophical', recur repeatedly throughout Laforgue's work: the impersonal cosmos, the essentially ephemeral nature of human experience, the physical city from which the poet is alienated observed from outside, and the psychological 'underwater' realities of the 'songeur'.

The consolations of religion are denied in this anonymous universe. Faith has lost its significance and the 'Eternity' of the prophets is replaced by the 'Eternullité' of the poet (l. 60). (This neologism was, incidentally, added to the poem when Laforgue was correcting the proofs.) Laforgue indulged himself in the inversion of generally accepted religious concepts. The spiritual staging points of modern man's progress through the world are those not of the soul but of Consciousness: 'des calvaires de la Conscience' (l. 53). The passion of Christ leads not to religious understanding but to Resignation—the inherited, simplified buddhist type of acceptance where comprehension is impossible. The spiritual insights sought or desired in Galathea are in fact simply generated by the fact of birth and beyond the level of desire, such is the implication, have no meaning: 'O Galathée aux pommiers de l'Eden-Natal'. In this quatrain (ll. 53–6), 'Idéal' is a Hartmann word which refers back to the impersonal, unattainable, 'Everything', the Brahma 'Tout-Un en soi'. But modern man, the poet, can no more attune himself to these natural actualities than to the religious rites celebrated this Christmas Eve. Of these frustrating dilemmas he consequently washes his hands: 'Maintenant, je m'en lave les mains' and accepts his dependence on universal laws that are beyond his understanding. He cannot understand, but would rather believe in them than be a dupe to the mere processes of existence. It is in this sense that he said elsewhere Hartmann's *Philosophie de l'Inconscient* was his bible: 'Moi...Je la veux cuver au sein de l'INCONSCIENT' (l. 104). The notion that the fundamental meaninglessness of normal life justifies the poet's sense of alienation from it is central in Laforgue. Here it is expressed explicitly in the heavy rhetoric of his early philosophical poems, but when he moves beyond this type of rhetoric it remains a powerful, implicit, imaginative determinant which he never abandoned. Laforgue obviously realized this when he resolved to retain the poem.

Stylistically, the poem is unsuccessful. Often quoted is Laforgue's letter to his sister dated, conjecturally, May 1883:

> Je trouve stupide de faire la grosse voix et de jouer de l'éloquence. Aujourd'hui que je suis plus sceptique et que je m'emballe moins aisément et que, d'autre part, je possède ma langue d'une façon plus minutieuse, plus clownesque, j'écris de petits poèmes de fantaisie, n'ayant qu'un but: faire de l'original à tout prix.

This he indeed managed to do in 1883. The rhetoric or 'high tone' of 'Préludes Autobiographiques', its preference for concept rather than metaphor, its declamatory phrasing, its unequal, sometimes inelegant alexandrines that carry nonetheless ancient resonances inappropriate to Laforgue's immediate purposes, its unconvincing dramatic structure in which a walk on Christmas Eve through the streets of Paris is made to support such a weight of metaphysics,—all this Laforgue abandoned when he conceived his new kind of poem. In short, 'Préludes Autobiographiques' is not a genuine 'Complainte' at all and the reader who is sympathetic to the immense inventiveness and vitality of the better poems is obliged to endorse the opinion of Laforgue's friends that he ought to have omitted it.

COMPLAINTE PROPITIATOIRE A L'INCONSCIENT

Whatever its date of composition, this poem serves the same function as 'Préludes Autobiographiques' in establishing the poetic terms of reference for the collection as a whole. Once again it is easy to see that it relates to early prose notes like the following heady passage reprinted in *Mélanges Posthumes*: 'Le Sage de l'humanité nouvelle. Catéchisme pessimiste— Absurdités des remèdes. Deux solutions proposées: Bouddha, l'Inde vénérable—Schopenhauer, Hartmann. Pas de remède absolu, universel, qui supprime le mal universel...Il faut se contenter du suicide matériel et du renoncement. Tuez votre existence individuelle, matériellement ou intellectuellement, mais ne songez pas à tuer le Vouloir universel.' The universal Will is in the poem addressed as 'Aditi', a goddess and mother figure who represents the Vedic Universal Being. In the mock prayer which constitutes half of the poem (the six couplets), the poet asks to be delivered from Thought, for thought, intellectualizing, analysing, is seen as the disease which from the beginning caused man's troubles ('Lèpre originelle'), as an insane drunkenness, as the root of evil and of exile, where 'alienation' not literal exile is meant. Therefore the prayer is addressed to 'votre inconsciente Volonté': let us give up the idea that the individual thinking person is important is the implication and, instead, accept with resignation that the Earth is only a small and not necessarily an important part of the Universe.

There is, therefore, no point in pretending that affection in human relations is more than a transitory feeling: 'd'occasion'. The other part of the poem, the part in quatrains, concerns the futility and suffering of actual existence, the foolishness of the woman who says she will love forever, the irrelevance of suffering, the meaninglessness of being a man of the arts. There is a certain neatness in the way in which the two parts of the poem are balanced, but again it has to be concluded that Laforgue made a mistake in giving it this prominence in the volume. Too many readers would be either offended or bored by the heavy distortion of Christian words ('Eucharistie', 'la Pâque', and so on) and by the heavy humour. For the first type of person, the poem was a blatant, frontal attack on orthodox belief. For the second it was a dwelling on the obvious. It was exactly this extravagance of conception, as well as the extravagance of wording ('Lèpre originelle' and similar phrases) that Laforgue abandoned when he began to write the real 'Complaintes' in 1883.

COMPLAINTE-PLACET DE FAUST FILS

Here 'maman Nature' has the same function as the Universal Will, the 'Tout', the Unconscious of the preceding poems and the four stanza lyric is in fact a variation on the themes already discussed in 'Préludes Autobiographiques'.

Note that in this edition the word 'puis' is retained as consistent with the poem (though altered in some other editions) and that Laforgue's capitalized 'Je' is also kept as an unaccidental typographical idiosyncrasy which Laforgue consistently retained when he proof read.

COMPLAINTE A NOTRE-DAME DES SOIRS

Probably the last of the group of early poems at the beginning of the volume (again a reference to 'mes vingt ans') but perhaps re-written or tidied up after 1883, this poem too depends upon an inversion of expected meaning. The actual cathedral of *Notre-Dame* which had evidently moved and fascinated the young Laforgue is replaced by the sky itself, the night sky, the sky of universal presences where the moon shines equally on a Christian Cathedral in Paris and 'La Mecque'. By contrast, the sun represents the processes of Nature, generation, sex, decay. Nature is a 'Usine de sève', a mere factory for making the liquids upon which vegetable growth depends and the result, the harvest, is the round of generation and sexuality: 'Puis retournent à ces vendanges sexciproques'. The sun, which causes all this, rears up, bleeds to death, is crucified. (We can note in passing that this sun-moon opposition is sustained throughout Laforgue's work. It is the same sun which dies in 'L'Hiver qui Vient' in *Derniers Vers* and the same moon that Pierrot celebrates in *L'Imitation de Notre-Dame la Lune*. The sun stands for unthinking acceptance of the meaningless biological processes by which life is maintained. The moon stands for the cold world of the intellect which realizes negating nature is the only guarantee of individual existence.) This sun has died many times in sunset, over the waters which rock and nurse the poet's sailing boat, in the moonlight where meditation and communion with the Universal become possible. As in 'Préludes Autobiographiques' the water, the sea, 'les lacs' of this poem symbolize the Unconscious through which the poet can drift and such drifting, for a Nihilist, is more meaningful than living with a purpose in the day's sunlight.

The internal counterpoint of this poem is perhaps not wholly worked out. The line 'Ah! coquette Marie', despite the religious overtone, seems to refer to an actual person. 'Maman Nature', however, 'Notre-Dame des Soirs', is not fickle and coquettish. With her a rendezvous must happen: 'De *vrais* yeux m'ont dit: au revoir!' By contrast, actual human rendezvous are mocked or despised: 'Et moi, moi Je m'en moque!'— that is, he affects to despise the sexual torments that lead people 'Pour un regard' to beat their heads on the pavement or be overcome, 'suffocated', in an ecstasy of adoration. If something of this kind is in the poem, it is not fully realized: only when Laforgue left behind him these vast oppositions between traditional belief as represented by the Church and an anarchic faith in intellectual liberty as represented by the poses and stances of the Nihilist did he learn to write a genuinely psychological poem.

'Complainte à Notre-Dame des Soirs' is for all that a more intriguing poem than the ones which preceded it. Its lines do not echo with other poets' sounds, its seven line stanza is deftly accomplished, its internal tonal resonance is more finely tuned. Though some of the verbal effects are superficial (like the incipient pun in 'couchants' and the extraordinarily barbaric neologism 'sexciproques') and some a little unconvincing (like the sea-earth transposition in 'En voyage, sur les fugitives prairies'), the poem has a greater verbal control than 'Préludes Autobiographiques', which was more a set of verse notes than a poem. In addition, of course, it plays its part in establishing the metaphorical boundaries of the poems which follow.

Note that, although Laforgue told Charles Henry that he had altered 'sexciproques' in proof, there is no textual or bibliographical evidence that he did so.

COMPLAINTE DES VOIX SOUS LE FIGUIER BOUDDHIQUE

The spelling of 'Boudhique' in the first edition title was a print-shop error. There may have been others. The table of contents page of the first edition carried the erratum: 'Page 21 lire: Au lieu de sangsuelles... sensuelles.' Critics have speculated that this erratum was introduced not by Laforgue but by a bemused publisher. Certainly there was little point in his changing 'sangsuelles' if other neologisms like 'Eternullité' and 'sexciproques' were allowed to remain.

There is a significant difference between the first edition text of this poem and that of the uncorrected proof. Debauve usefully reprints the proof version verbatim from l. 45 to the end (*Debauve*, pp. 149–50). There is no firm evidence of when the poem was written but the title, the recurring imagery which relates it to the preceding poems and the 'cosmic consciousness' indicate that it was in 1880. The revisions were made, of course, in 1885 and were referred to in a letter to Vanier: 'Je vous renvoie ces épreuves. Vous verrez que j'ai beaucoup ajouté à la pièce *les voix* etc. pour moi la plus importante (significative) en un sens du volume—J'ai numéroté la série des distiques pour l'ordre dans lequel ils seront placés.—J'espère qu'on se tirera d'affaire. Une erreur dans cette pièce me désolerait (*Debauve.* p. 95). It is interesting to have such a clear case of revision without an intervening 1883 version. In proof, Laforgue added ll. 49–52, 65–79 and 91–5. They are tightly written, bitterly worded additions arching over, as it were, the vivacity of the 'Complaintes' written in 1883. If, in 1880, he wrote lines like:

> Et tes pudeurs ne sont que des passes réflexes
>
> Dont joue un Dieu très fort (Ministère des sexes)

and then in 1885 added, for example, that the sentimental fingers of the Eternal Feminine which caress the young constitute 'des trouvailles d'animal', not much, obviously, had changed. Here is a harsh rejection of woman where sex is dismissed as a trick, a falseness, a drug. The young are deceived by it into complicity in the animal 'functions' of existence but the comment of 'Le figuier' is:

Pauvres fous, vraiment pauvres fous!

This line of critical speculation reinforces the idea that there remained a great difference between the burst of creative energy which produced the 'Complaintes' of 1883 and the more dogged, less creative making of poems for the sake of book publication.

COMPLAINTE DE CETTE BONNE LUNE

At last the reader comes to a poem with a lighter tone, which is obviously written with the sounds of a popular song in mind. While the earth rotates a dialogue between the moon and stars is imagined. The moon is attached to the earth, is faithful to her 'sister planet'. The stars try to woo her away because the earth is 'un suppôt / De la Pensée' but they fail and eventually dismiss her as 'rosière enfarinée' and 'metteuse en rut des vieux matous'. This light treatment of themes and images that had always fascinated Laforgue reminds one more of the Pierrot poem in *L'Imitation de Notre-Dame la Lune* than the genuine 'Complaintes' which follow it.

COMPLAINTE DES PIANOS QU'ON ENTEND DANS LES QUARTIERS AISES

Laforgue noted in the copy he gave his sister that this poem was written in Paris in 1883. The *Agenda* entry dates it as 12 May 1883. The difference between the didactic, heavily stressed, high-toned early poems and the fractured, lighter, less aggressive nature of this one will be perfectly clear. The reader will decide for himself whether the couplets turned by neat rhymes (the technique Eliot imitated), the counterpoint achieved by the interweaving of stanzas with different imaginative weight and different line length, and the questioning, quizzical, ironical, inconclusive tone of the whole, represent a decadence out of control, with meaning literally abandoned or fractured, or whether Laforgue has found for himself the type of artistic freedom discussed in the Introduction. Certainly more is now done by the juxtaposition and association of poetic ideas than by argument and the irony is lighter, less dependent upon the iconoclastic inversion of orthodox meaning that Laforgue indulged in during his pre-German days.

Piano music heard in the streets of middle-class districts of the city is a recurring symbol in Laforgue, both for the meaninglessness of bourgeois existence (on and on and on these comfortably placed young girls

play their Chopin) and for the sense of alienation the person outside
must feel. Several passages reprinted in *Mélanges Posthumes*, for example,
convey the sort of thing Laforgue had in mind: 'Quelle est cette rue de
province aisée? A une fenêtre, des rideaux, un piano travaille réglé d'un
métronome cette eternelle valse de Chopin usée comme l'Amour' (*MP*,
p. 30). Here, in this poem, 'Premiers soirs, sans pardessus' because it is
May; 'chaste flânerie' because the young 'outsider' who has been
brought up on books ('que les Lettres ont bien nourrie') merely wanders
about the streets by himself, his nerves, his feelings, 'broken' or not
understood. The full line reads:

> Aux complaintes des nerfs incompris et brisés

and this to a great extent is what a 'Complainte' is: a lament which
derives from the sensations of loneliness, meaninglessness, fracture,
disintegration. The emphasis is upon 'des nerfs', the psychological
responses of someone who is alienated, who is affected by what he
thinks, sees, experiences, but who cannot make sense of life, as opposed
to the assertions of the early poems where ideas not sensations were
dominant. The shift from the argumentative to the psychological gives
Laforgue the chance to write this new type of poem, where the unity is
not that of argument but of the association and counterpoint of images.

Do the girls indoors dream of Romantic heroes, 'A des Roland', the
poet wonders—of Romantic heroes fit for bourgeois domestication, 'à
des dentelles?' If so, they are part of the inevitable round of existence,
part of the actual world of boarding houses, theatres, newspapers,
novels, part of 'le bal incessant de nos étranges rues', and as such
vulnerable to those seasonal, May-time, biological resurgences by which
the world mechanically keeps itself going, 'aux hérédités en ponctuels
ferments', just as they are vulnerable to the seductive piano music that
deceives them into a belief in what they are doing. All this is inevitable
and is inevitably dismissed:

> Allez, stériles ritournelles,
> La vie est vraie et criminelle.

Life is criminal because it deceives human beings into believing in it.
But it is true: this is how it actually is, an eternal round, a 'ritournelle',
an actual sterility despite the 'ponctuels ferments' of sexual passion and
generation.

Later in the poem this idea is repeated, but with greater irony:

> La vie est là: le pur flacon des vives gouttes
> Sera, *comme il convient*, d'eau propre baptisé.

From this the perverse, alienated poet dissociates himself. To him the
spirit of the impersonal, of the Unconscious, will return:

> Mais tu nous reviendras bien vite
> Guérir mon beau mal, n'est-ce pas?

In a hostile reading of the poem, a phrase like 'mon beau mal' might be seen as representing the poet's or the fictional persona's basic confusion. Shall he participate or shall he not? If not, why the anxiety and why the angry irony at the expense of the bourgeois? If yes, why the confusion between the loneliness of the outsider and his apparent lack of self-knowledge? A more sympathetic reading will allow this very confusion, represented as it is by the unresolved tensions of the poem, to be part of the condition of alienation. In any case, the poem is distinctly different from the ones that precede it. In form it is analogous, in its shifts of tone and emphasis and rhythm, to that piano music heard 'dans les quartiers aisés'. Its drift, its character, is more artistic, much less didactic.

COMPLAINTE DE LA BONNE DEFUNTE

This simple lyric scarcely needs comment or explanation. With this poem in mind, though, one might reconsider the insistence of the effect of woman's eyes in other poems, particularly the early ones. Here we have 'Yeux désolés' and 'Yeux trop mûrs', the eyes which seduce and distract. Perhaps this is what Laforgue always had in mind, inveterate *flâneur* that he was.

COMPLAINTE DE L'ORGUE DE BARBARIE

The damage done when Laforgue expanded 'Complainte des Voix' can most easily be noted at this point in the volume. Trézenick had to rearrange, re-set and partly re-paginate the first four sheets in order to accommodate the poet's last minute decision to add a page. That this occurred after Laforgue had seen the first batch of proofs is clear from the fact that on one of the sets in Debauve's possession the page number 32 is corrected to 33. Incidentally, Vanier accepted Laforgue's offer to pay for the large amount of correction and emendation at this stage.

Laforgue again adopts the structure by which two stanzas at the beginning and end of the poem, conjuring up the sound of the barrel organ, encase two sets of alternating stanzas representing a dialogue, as it were, between people with different points of view, albeit imaginary people like the 'Let us go then you and I' of Eliot's poem. One set, in quatrains, concerns the paraphernalia of human existence, the 'Mortels postiches' or material superfluities, like gas light, billboards, piano music, the novels to be bought on the *quais*, photographs, slippers, clogs and so forth. In this world, the woman, Eve, is faithful—like a vegetable. The man is not. But to the sound of the organ couples drink beer and dance. Life is like a sudden agitation ('un coup de balai') or the dismal process of consumption and excretion ('Des berceaux fienteux'). Once again, Laforgue is neat, concise, cynical, destructive.

The other set of stanzas, the couplets, seems to refer to something more immediate and personal: a journey through the autumn woods at night. The proper name in the line 'Paul, ce bois est mal famé' has an enigmatic effect, as indeed unidentifiable proper names often have.

An ambitious poem to the extent that Laforgue attempted to achieve a great deal in a small compass, it does not quite succeed, because the words seem to refer to a situation which can never be completely visualized. 'O ballets corrosifs! réel, le crime?', probably the crucial line, is impenetrable. One way of seeing this would be to compare the poem to the later 'Solo de Lune' in *Derniers Vers* in which the ride through the autumn woods is fully imagined and the counterpoint between the particular and the general more adequately handled.

COMPLAINTE D'UN CERTAIN DIMANCHE and COMPLAINTE D'UN AUTRE DIMANCHE

The idea of Sunday was an ambivalent one for Laforgue. It was the day on which he did not have to read and he was consequently free for excursions. Fairly clearly many of these Sundays or abbreviated week-ends were spent with women. Sunday, at the same time, was the image for those bourgeois inanities he affected to despise: churchgoing, dull afternoons at home, parading the town in one's best clothes, boredom, ennui, piano music. A very large number of published and unpublished prose passages express the sentiments of the following comment taken from *Mélanges Posthumes*: 'Voilà qu'on entend quelques cloches d'après les vêpres disant la province bloquée sans espoir et les dimanches de vieilles filles (*MP*, p. 30).

In 1883 some of these Sundays were spent with R and this may have been one. Conceived in Coblenz in July 1883, it was quite obviously written on a particular occasion and is completely different from the preceding poems for this reason. Those poems were largely verbal and intellectual, positively preventing, except for the odd hint, any speculation about the experiences which might have informed them, if there were such experiences. Here, the occasion is stated. The poet has spent the day and probably the previous night or nights in a hotel overlooking the Rhine, has been down to the river to see her off by boat and now has his evening meal by himself, sad to be alone but puzzled to be sad.

The simplicity of the second stanza is a new element: he meets the village children on their way to the baker's and back in his hotel he feeds bread to the sparrows. On Sunday the children go to have the 'tièdes brioches' blessed; the sparrows, imagined as 'des âmes d'amis morts', fly away 'comme blessés'. The neatness and simplicity of this parallel gives point to the refrain

> Ah! jusqu'à ce que la nature soit bien bonne

as well as to that important concluding line which is so startlingly different from the way in which Laforgue had been writing up to this point:

> O mes humains, consolons-nous les uns les autres.

The habit of cynicism has been relaxed, at least slightly. The gnats, the ephemera, dance about in the rays of the setting sun and expire in the rooftop heat of houses where supper is being prepared. The poet has been disturbed: not now 'Je veux' but 'Faudra-t-il vivre monotone'.

The way in which the poet by himself reflects upon this experience is still somewhat high-toned, rhetorical, 'philosophical'. It is not an ordinary person who hopes for something more significant than the sexual, but 'l'Etre'; his dreams are overcome by 'Le Spleen, eunuque à froid'. Yet these ideas are not empty abstractions but are informed by the actuality of the departure that the poem describes, and in particular by the second and third stanzas. The balance works and the poem is self-contained.

The companion piece, 'Complainte d'un Autre Dimanche', was written in Paris in October 1884, according to Laforgue's notation in his sister's copy. A companion piece by title and position, it concerns the recollection, in a different and distant hotel room, of a time, a Sunday, which was not completely lonely.

> Quoi! la vie est unique, et toi, sous ce scaphandre,
> Tu te racontes sans fin, et tu te ressasses!
> Seras-tu donc toujours un qui garde la chambre?

This does much to balance the verbal extravagance of the previous three stanzas.

Most readers of Laforgue will find it natural to compare these two poems with the two later 'Dimanches' poems in *Derniers Vers*.

COMPLAINTE DU FŒTUS DE POETE

Concerning this squib, which is about the progress of the child at birth from the womb to its mother's breast, Laforgue wrote to Kahn: 'Est-ce assez idiot au fond? Que pensez-vous du vers de onze pieds? et par la même occasion, que pensez-vous aussi de l'infini?' (*LA*, p. 55). It will serve here as an example of a poem which Laforgue evidently liked and which was revised at least twice, for he noted the date of composition in the *Agenda* as March 1883 and probably re-wrote it when he sent a copy to Kahn in 1884. Since the version sent to Kahn is different from the first edition text, he must have re-written the poem during the winter of 1884–5, or conceivably at the proof stage, because only two sets of uncorrected proofs have survived.

For interest's sake, here is the text of the poem as sent to Gustave Kahn:

> En avant! en avant!
> Déchirer la nuit gluante des racines!
> A travers l'Amour, Océan d'albumine,
> Vers le soleil, vers l'alme et vaste étamine
> Du soleil levant!
>
> En avant!
> A travers le sang gras d'amour, à la nage,
> Têter le Soleil! et soûl de lait, bavant
> Dodo sur les seins dorloteurs des nuages
> Voyageurs mouvants!
>
> En avant!
> Galop sur les seins dorloteurs des nuages,
> Dans la main de Dieu, bleue aux mille yeux vivants,
> Au pays du lait tiède faire naufrage...
> —Courage!
> Là, là, je me dégage...
>
> En avant!
> Geins, douce prison! Filtre soleil torride!
> Ma nuit, je ne puis gicler que vous crevant.
> Donc, fanez-vous en loques ma chrysalide,
> —Non, j'ai froid?...En avant
> —Ah! maman.

Not every poet in 1885 would dare to refer to the breaking of the child from its mother's womb ('la nuit gluante des racines'), to its emancipation, to the mucus of childbirth ('sauvé des steppes de mucus'), or to the pubic hair over the mother's womb ('forêts d'aquarium'), or to be so frivolous in imagining the child's first experiences, the birth between another's legs, the sudden breath of cold air, the first sight of the material world ('Cogne, glas des nuits! filtre, soleil solide!') In a society in which even the word 'fœtus' was regarded with alarm, this uncompromising, unsentimental treatment of childbirth was calculated to offend, or rather, as in this poem, to amuse by its contrived offen-siveness. 'Un livre fou', said an early reviewer in the November 1886 issue of *La Revue littéraire et artistique*, 'plus décadent que les décadents et plus détraqué que les détraqués.—Ce serait triste, si ce n'était drôle, d'autant plus que c'est sérieux, oui, en vérité très sérieux. L'auteur a cru sentir ce qu'il écrit. O Paul Verlaine, ô Mallarmé, voilà quelle race vous faites!'

COMPLAINTE DES PUBERTES DIFFICILES

Marie Laforgue's copy has the notation: 'Sept. 1882. 99 Boulv. St. Michel'.

Another hotel poem. The poet inspects a jade elephant and a china or porcelain vase. The elephant is a 'Bon bouddha' indifferent to immediate anguish and suffering. The design on the vase depicts a pastoral paradise in which a couple of shepherds are transfixed 'jusqu'au trépas', for ever on the point of consummating their love, while the figure of Pan watches unconcernedly, 'ses bras tout inconscients'. Actually these lovers are entrapped in the 'sot Eden de Florian' and are 'impuissant d'opéra', that is more like characters in a fiction than real people. By contrast the poet, or the 'lui' of the poem, sits by himself listening to the happy voices beneath him thinking, in a rage of suffering, of his own neglected talent. 'J'ai du génie, enfin: nulle ne veut m'aimer!'

COMPLAINTE DE LA FIN DES JOURNEES

A rather uninspiring poem which plays on the ideas expressed with greater liveliness and power in many others: the sense of personal loneliness ('Oh! qui veut visiter les palais de mes sens'), the foolishness of existence (he is 'follement solitaire'), the transitory quality of exper-iences which lead routinely to death, and the necessity of accepting what can never be fully understood ('Inconsciente Loi'). The image of Philoctetes, left by himself on an island while his companions go into action, is scarcely vibrant with originality. Self-pity, for example the fear of not being understood, is a heavy weight for a poem to bear unless it contains more of the occasion of feeling, or the cause, than this poem does.

Debauve notes the existence of a sale catalogue in which a manuscript of this poem was reproduced (Debauve, p. 34); he himself possesses a different manuscript, as well as lightly corrected proof sheets (which incidentally gave the amusing reading of 'Poire' instead of 'Foire' in the penultimate line). Unfortunately, these documents do not help us to date the poem; nor are they of very great critical interest, except for the detail that the word 'grêle' was added to l. 11 during proof reading. Several errors in the text were not corrected.

COMPLAINTE DE LA VIGIE AUX MINUITS POLAIRES
and COMPLAINTE DE LA LUNE EN PROVINCE

Two slight lyrics which, given Laforgue's idiosyncratic poetic idiom, scarcely need detailed exegesis.

The first, 'Complainte de la Vigie aux Minuits polaires', is an example of what happened when Laforgue failed to 'realize' a poetic conception in a precise way. He was not, of course, in any sense a Symbolist. His poems always refer either to actual experiences, however remotely, or to intellectual predicaments and the emotions associated with them. Normally, what saves him from being merely descriptive or merely intellectual is his wit which, together with immense verbal virtuosity, allows him to make poems which chart the limits of his consciousness or self-consciousness on a particular occasion, for a particular poem. Rarely does this take the form of a poem in which the image dominates the word; it is usually the word which controls the image. This means that without considerable verbal originality his poems tend to fall flat. This is the case with 'Complaintes de la Vigie aux Minuits Polaires' where nothing occurs to ignite what for Laforgue is his stock vocabulary for a lament: 'sanglots', 'un beau cœur', 'Se meurt, de ne pouvoir / Saigner' and so on. One is therefore left with a slight lyric *à la mode de Laforgue* which lacks memorable features and which at the end degenerates into bathos.

The second in this pair of lyrics, 'Complainte de la Lune en Province', is even more light-weight, being little more than a flight of fancy on the theme of the moon. Deep in the provinces the poet dies (with boredom?) and the moon, representative of the Cosmic, ignores him with 'Du coton dans les oreilles'. This reads like a very early poem, but the date of composition is not known.

COMPLAINTE DES PRINTEMPS
and COMPLAINTE DE L'AUTOMNE MONOTONE

These two poems, in all likelihood written in 1883 and placed together in the volume, are as it were typical 'Complaintes' in their fractured form, in the verve of counterpoint, in what might be called their poetic impudence and in the fact that they both constitute a treatment of familiar ideas—ideas which become very familiar, that is, to a reader of this volume. Thus, spring is that unromantic season in which the 'system' operates 'Avec son impudent cortège d'excitants', while the autumn is the season when the sun dies and life dies with it. The poet is detached from the totality of the experience. In 'Complainte des Printemps' he is detached from the new life that comes with spring (ll. 14–16). In 'Complainte de l'Automne monotone', he reflects upon the sun's failure: 'Il se crut incompris'. In both poems, Laforgue utilizes the structure of alternating stanzas in which one set is song-like, with short lines and simple, though sometimes wildly unconventional rhymes.

Laforgue almost invariably became over-excited about sexuality, especially when he saw it as a somewhat brutish physiological process quite in opposition to Romantic notions of ideal love. As mentioned earlier, the understanding that it was a process was part of his decadence: how could a sensible person attach value to masculine-femine attachments that had merely to do with instinct and reflex? Psychological explanations have sometimes been offered for this obsession. People speculate, for instance, that Laforgue was profoundly upset by the death of his mother in childbirth; others, that Laforgue's own need of love, and the sexual frustrations or repressions that were a concomitant feature of sustained periods of loneliness and isolation, together made him not only bitter, but also somewhat too unyielding in his Nihilist rejection of what others took for granted. These genetic considerations are mentioned here incidentally: they do not of course affect the literary value of the poems.

The startlingly contrived rhyme of ll. 29–30 seems harsh, and as representative of a habit of mind becomes perhaps a rather wearisome trick of style.

Two minor points concerning 'Complainte des Printemps'. First, it is interesting to note that when Laforgue corrected the proof he eliminated some of the more colloquial lines. Debauve (p. 154) reprints, for example, the original version of ll. 25–8:

> V'là que la p'tite est pleine!
> Drôle de phénomène...
> Ça me fait bien d'la peine,
> Mais j'eus assez d'ma bidaine.

No doubt Laforgue had to re-write this and similar passages in order to satisfy his Paris friends and his publisher. (Writing of this kind dates the poem to Laforgue's high-spirited spring in 1883, by the way.) Second, the final lines are a little puzzling, since they would so much more easily fit into an autumn than a spring poem. Maybe it is not too ungenerous to regard this as a clue to the way Laforgue assembled and re-assembled his poems?

'Complainte de l'Automne' is a seasonal poem which associates the loss of love ('Nulle ne songe à m'aimer un peu') with the end of the year which seems like the end of life. Detail makes this a better poem than 'Complaintes des Printemps', but for all that it has to be regarded as an anticipation of other, stronger poems about autumn sickness (such as 'Complainte d'une Convalescence') and, equally important, as an early draft of several passages in *Derniers Vers*. A reader new to Laforgue might wish to compare it with the first and the last of the *Derniers Vers*, because by doing so he would be able to judge for himself to what extent individual poems in *Les Complaintes* were fully fashioned and independent and to what extent they simply mark his progress towards his last book, which was his most important poetic achievement.

The last four lines, which undoubtedly improve the poem, were added at the proof correction stage.

COMPLAINTE DE L'ANGE INCURABLE

Laforgue corrected the printing error of 'L'Angle' instead of 'L'Ange' in the title in the presentation copies given to Marie Laforgue and Laurent Tailhade, having missed it at the proof stage. In his sister's copy he noted it had been written in Berlin during the winter.

Yet another lament for lost or consummated love, 'Complainte de l'Ange incurable', though written in Berlin, evokes the atmosphere of the low countries where a lonely knight-at-arms, 'diaphane d'amour', rides amongst the still windmills whose arms are still and bare. Again the alternating stanza patterns, here linked in sets of six lines by the rhyme. Again regret from the springtime of love, for the time which has passed. And again the evocation of autumn, the frozen pools, the wagtail by the frozen water's edge, the bare hillsides.

Clearly this is a less bitter poem than many of the others. 'Vivre est encore le meilleur parti ici-bas', the poet says. The regret for the lost love seems genuine or at least is not undercut by irony: 'où sans châle tu vas'. (Compare this, though, with the same idea expressed in a slightly different way in the final lines of 'Solo de Lune' in *Derniers Vers*.) The sails of the windmills, 'les ailes', the phantom shapes which confuse the vision of the 'Chevalier-Errant' giving him Romantic ideas which experience does not justify are contrasted with the wings of the human angel, 'des ailes / D'Hostie ivre et ravie aux cités sensuelles!' where 'Hostie' seems to stand not for anything religious but for 'victim of circumstance' or the unliberated existence 'ivre et ravie aux cités sensuelles!' However, there is another contrast in this part of the poem, the contrast between 'vaisselles / D'ici-bas!' representing on the one side acceptance of the mundane and, on the other, the wings which theoretically ought to allow freedom but which in fact do not: 'des ailes / A jamais!' In this contrast the cynical, sexual implication in the line 'Serrez ces mains sauçant dans de vagues vaisselles!' is balanced by the ironical inconclusiveness of the conclusion:

> —Tant il est vrai que la saison dite d'automne
> N'est aux cœurs mal fichus rien moins que folichonne.

Despite the inconclusiveness, these contrasting sets of ideas are in fact dominated by the over-riding pessimism of the poem, a pessimism all the more certain for the poem being a good one. Inevitably the poet who suffers lacks consolation: 'Ni Dieu, ni l'art, ni ma Sœur Fidèle'. Rather, his vision of life is captured in images like that extraordinarily unsettling one in ll. 15–16:

> Un trou, qu'asperge un prêtre âgé qui se morfond,
> Bâille à ce libéré de l'être;...

Yet this dominant tone of pessimism is itself moderated by a characteristically melancholy theme: 'Sais-tu bien, folle pure, où sans châle tu vas?' he asks the lover who leaves him.

COMPLAINTES DES NOSTALGIES PREHISTORIQUES

Laforgue *felt* alienated: the feeling was a fact of his experience and he never overcame it. The feeling was expressed in a number of ways: remorse, self-pity, sorrow, disdain. In the more interesting poems there is an amalgam of feeling representing an ironical, detached but not insensitive appreciation of man's predicament. In less successful poems, Laforgue gives way to extremes of bitterness or self-pity which seem callow. The feeling of being alienated is, after all, genuine enough, even though not shared universally, but ideas which derive from the feeling are more suspect. Here is an extremist poem whose internal logic is suspect. A man dines and while he eats reflects on his environment. He calls these reflections 'nostalgies' because he drifts backwards into the real world from which a sophisticated intellectual would normally be detached. He calls the reflections 'préhistoriques' because real life is primitive by comparison with a more finely tuned appreciation of the ultimate meaninglessness of actuality. Thus a high premium is placed on sensibility which does not celebrate but negates ordinary life.

The snobbery and elitism of this position were not accidental. Take, for example, the following prose note which was reprinted in *Mélanges*

Posthumes. With the high tone of the adolescent dogmatist, Laforgue wrote about what a buddhist resignation entailed:

> Avant d'arriver au renoncement, il faut souffrir au moins deux ans: jeûner, souffrir de la continence, saigner de pitié et d'amour universel, visiter les hôpitaux, toutes les maladies hideuses ou tristes...

All well and good, one thinks, despite the high and mighty tone. But this passage about what Laforgue called a 'remedy' that might be adopted by the individual was preceded by this paragraph:

> Ce remède, je ne le sais que trop, ne peut être, du moins encore, qu'à la portée d'une élite. Pour les autres, la charité, l'amour, l'instruction, l'émancipation, maintenir doucement dans l'illusion, ne provoquer le déchirement que lorsqu'on sait que l'individu peut être mûr pour cet état et peut arriver au renoncement. (*MP*, p. 11).

What Laforgue calls renunciation, and what others might call irresponsible callousness, is not only preferred to a life of commitment but is also a prior condition for a sensitive existence, for a life of the sensibility. To put it this way admittedly distorts what Laforgue obviously felt: he *felt* that a sense of alienation, an appreciation of art, a conviction about the essential futility of existence and the torment of loneliness were all integral features of the same condition. In this he was no doubt sincere. But if the ideas are taken seriously, they offend common sense. A person can devote himself to charity or be in love *and* be aware of the metaphysical problems that caused the young Laforgue so much anguish. This is to put the matter generously. An ungenerous account might place emphasis upon the artificiality of Laforgue's role in the household of the Empress Augusta, a position scarcely calculated to reduce or dampen the snobbery of the passage quoted above.

In 'Complainte des Nostalgies préhistoriques' it is evening time and the world is at its evening meal: 'On dîne'. Why does the sun-burnt child who is eating apricots in a valley of flowers have to be 'bestiale'? Why must the pleasure of an 'idylle' be either facile or furtive? Why in Laforgue are simple physical pleasures, like the pleasures of sex, invariably denied? Why is it always more important to be delivered from than to enjoy ecstasy? These queries underlie this brilliant poem. Mouths eat. Each mouth relishes ('sirote') its own pleasure. Distant mouths cry out with vitality—'voluptés à vif'—echoing the sounds of 'des grands soirs primitifs', when the beasts and Adam and Eve coupled. The mouth of the boy sucks the juice of the apricot with pleasure, with a 'primitive' or 'pre-historic' satisfaction. The sugary lips of the lover play over the 'corps de fruits' of his mistress with a similar satisfaction. It is the mouth which is primitive. It sucks, kisses, caresses, yawns. It is speechless: 'sans rien dire'. It laughs, foolishly, like the toads which, excited by the moonlight, begin to croak, while the lovers are released from their 'ecstasy'; beneath the moon 'Fous, nous renverser sur les reins'. Such are the pleasures of those misty towns when a man returns from work, 'mal repu des gains machinals'. Such are the pleasures of any couple which fails to emulate the indifferent moon who dines with art, unmasked, adopting an innocent 'imbécile' air 'parmi des vierges débiles', as though he can pretend not to be responsible for the lunacy of mankind. Life has gone on like this, under such a moon, since prehistoric days.

People who speak to each other when they make love, who prefer to share and prolong their sexual pleasures rather than be delivered from them, and who associate sex with mutual affection and companionship, may have difficulty in identifying with Laforgue's *fin-de-siecle* sentiments! On the other hand, they may enjoy the audacity of the poem, which for 1885 was considerable.

Incidentally, it should be clear from this discussion that Pascal Pia made a mistake in correcting 'délèvrant' to 'délivrant' in l. 26. The mouth imagery makes it obvious that Laforgue's coinage was deliberate. Pichois correctly removed the circumflex from 'juteux' in l. 15. Note that one of the proof corrections recorded by Debauve was the replacement of 'génie' in l. 8 by 'gésine'. The root sense of 'generation' in 'génie' was too remote: 'gésine', the place where a woman or an animal has her off-spring, relates metaphorically to 'couchants', one of Laforgue's favourite puns, and in the context of 'nostalgies préhistoriques' is tellingly appropriate.

AUTRE COMPLAINTE DE L'ORGUE DE BARBARIE

Laforgue's preoccupation with the plaintive sounds of the street organ, which he reproduces in the melancholy tonal repetitiveness of this poem, and with the sounds of the raging wind, which in many poems as well as this one represents a meaningless turbulence consistent with the turbulence of his own thoughts, in this poem, 'Autre Complainte de l'Orgue de Barbarie', results in a restructuring of, by this time, familiar ideas for the sake of the alternating stanza pattern of a light lyric. The poem consists of verbal fragments that, taken by themselves, would be incomprehensible. In stanza, 7, for example, the reader of *Les Complaintes* knows that 'Cultes' and 'Littératures' and 'Yeux chauds' are images of the ephemeral with the instability of any relationship with a woman, indeed with women generally, but if the language of the poem were not explained by other poems in the volume it is doubtful whether it would be self-supporting. Its main drift would be clear, naturally, but it would not contain within itself enough to justify its rather nervous,

6—LC * *

fragmented phrasing. Consequently it would seem merely verbal, or perhaps in the last analysis it is.

COMPLAINTE DU PAUVRE CHEVALIER-ERRANT

A more ambitious poem technically than many of the other 'Complaintes', the 'Complainte du pauvre Chevalier-Errant' sustains a difficult stanza pattern with sets of deliciously impudent rhymes, which one would hope even the most solidly educated nominalist would be forced to admire for their pure verve. Here self-pity is minimized; Laforgue's cynicism is by contrast allowed free rein—if free rein is the right expression for a poem whose verbal vitality is so overwhelming. Like so many Romantic and post-Romantic poems in which escape from necessity is imagined only to be denied, this one has the form or structure of a flight of fancy which is brought to an end by a return to normality and common-sense, but instead of Laforgue's flight being to an ethereal or magical world as it might have been in a poem by Lamartine or Keats, it is to the fantasy world of assignation and love-making. As usual in *Les Complaintes* the lovers are the worldly, male dilettante, who is far too sophisticated really to believe in love, and a naïvely innocent, pre-Raphaelite type of girl who is more an object of attention, a sex-object, than a participant. Round this familiar situation the verbal structure of the poem is built.

It is a measure of the extent to which Laforgue has been unjustly neglected that those of his poems which patronisingly assume masculine superiority have escaped even the attention of the Feminist movement. A man who loved Laforgue's better poems more than he loved women might well choose to keep 'Complainte du pauvre Chevalier-Errant' to himself. If this seems improbable, he might protect the poem with the argument that emancipation from the bourgeois fear and guilt patterns associated with sexuality *ought* to have come in 1885 and that, if it had, the erotic fantasizing of 'du pauvre Chevalier-Errant' would not have had to be merely masculine. This may seem improbable too. It is a way of saying that Laforgue had indeed liberated himself from the moral taboos associated with the relations between men and women, including their sexual relations. In this sense he was enlightened and *avant-garde*. On the other hand, like the majority of his contemporaries he only infrequently seemed to understand the possibility of equal relations between people, least of all between the sexes. In this sense, he was unenlightened and reactionary. This poem is a good illustration of his ambivalent position.

The palaces of the soul, which a young girl might and in a sense does enter, are imaginary. Lines 3–6 for example are entirely an extension or decoration of l. 2. The landings, stairways and labyrinthine corridors fill out the idea of 'des palais de mon âme' and this 'filling out' is not the extension which allows the poet to explore the metaphor's implications for any profound purpose, but is chiefly decorative. For this decorative technique to work, the phrasing has to be intrinsically interesting, at least at first. In this instance it is. Furthermore the reader is led from l. 2 to l. 6 by the rhythm of the poem which holds together the lines of varied length and by their rhyme. Typically, the verbal formulation is not so far-fetched that one cannot hear in the stanza the tread of an actual woman walking along the corridors of a palace to the poet's room and, typically, this quite remote interest is held in check by the interest of the words themselves, by the novelty of verbal combination, by the textural effects of this as of the subsequent stanzas. Laforgue keeps such tight control over the sound of a stanza that novelty is never allowed to run riot.

Within the palace of the poet's soul are his 'Dilettantismes'. He is captivated, as it were, within the palace. Instincts are aroused, look out into the world, assert themselves. There is reflection or meditation, memory, vain sorties into the hallways. But the dilettante actions of the dilettante knight-errant are laden with remorse: 'chargés de colliers de remords'.

The next six stanzas concern the imagined assignation, the fantasy liaison, of two people who encounter each other in this unreal world of the poet's imagination, in his palace. Whatever heavy Nihilism, whatever heavy self-pity might have weighted down some of his other poems, in this poem the pure vitality of invention, however preposterous, gives an almost irresistible momentum to the reader's movement through the poem. If in this connection one mentions the pure verve of lines 16–18, or the exuberance of coinages like 'Feu-d'artificeront', or the witty economy of lines like

> Tu condimentes mes piments mystiques,
> J'assaisonne tes saisons;
> Nous blasons,

or the bravura of the final stanza where the unsuccessful poet imagines himself parading as a sandwich man outside some restaurant or hotel to advertise it and where 'toutes s'en fichent!' preposterously is made to rhyme with '*sandwiche*', it is not for the sake of exegesis, since the verbal brilliance of the poem lies so much on the surface and is accessible to anyone who is alert to the play on words, but rather to emphasise Laforgue's mastery of the form he adopted for the 'Complaintes' on these occasions when he allowed himself to be uninhibited and high-spirited. The mastery was complete and this poem must rank as a piece of brilliantly creative writing, whether the reader is attracted or repelled by the decadence of its chiefly verbal and textural effects.

COMPLAINTE DES FORMALITES NUPTIALES

This strange poem was first written in 1883, as noted in the *Agenda*, and then re-written at the proof-reading stage in 1885. The strangeness derives from the element of parody. The dialogue between 'Lui' and 'Elle', the echoing sound of some of the twelve syllable lines, and the affectedly archaic language of parts of the poem parody the 'high style' of neo-classical writers like Corneille and Racine. Laforgue makes fun of this high style by irony and anti-climax. The bathos of anti-climax is obvious:

> Et je le veux, de tout l'univers de mon être!
> Dis, veux-tu?

The irony is equally obvious, especially in the mock heroic lines like 'Tes yeux se font mortels, mais ton destin m'appelle'. 'Destin' indeed! The poem is full of these neo-classical words, used facetiously.

By contrast, the palace of this anti-hero contains not grand apartments but dictionaries, photographs, water, fruit, tobacco. It is the bachelor apartment of just an ordinary man bent on seducing his visitor, not the palace of a Greek hero, and in it there will not be the struggles of kinship and political rivalry but

> Les orgues de mes sens se feront vos martyrs
> Vers des cieux sans échos étoilés à mourir!

The cynically manipulated drama between the naïve girl, 'Oui, tes yeux francs seront désormais mon église', and the agreeably wicked lover

> Et tu t'éveilleras
> Guérie enfin du mal de pousser solitaire

is developed as a pastiche of such encounters in neo-classical drama. This is the sort of thing that actually goes on, says Laforgue.

Interesting changes were made to the poem in proof. The lines 32–5, 44–5 and 67 were added at that point. Lines 40–3 were entirely re-written. 'Croix' replaced 'beauté' in l. 15 and 'singulièrement' replaced 'douleureusement' in l. 18. In the proof, l. 21 read 'De l'eau, des fruits, de l'opium' and rhymed with l. 24, 'Et quelle imagination'. It seems a pity that Laforgue felt he had to replace 'de l'opium', a detail which obviously adds to the decadent atmosphere of the poem. Perhaps he found himself under pressure to do so. Though, with this exception, none of the changes is remarkable, the re-writing or restructuring strengthened the poem. It was no less light hearted and cynical as re-written, but more point was given to the dialogue as a whole when

Laforgue filled out what we have to call the main speech. Though relationships between men and women are ultimately meaningless and though a woman who craves to be a woman will in fact lose herself in her immemorial role

> Pour être, à son tour,
> Dame d'atour
> De Maïa!

he will nonetheless caress her 'singulièrement' and teach her to gather comfort

> Dans les jardins
> De nos instincts.

COMPLAINTE DES BLACKBOULES

By Laforgue's standards, this outburst of splenetic indignation is unusual. The woman to whom he proposed one Sunday while the orchestra played in the garden wants neither him nor his art. They blackball each other, she by rejecting him, he by imagining a grotesque retaliation which is luridly described in stanzas 5–9. She is to be incarcerated as a mad woman ('parmi de vagues folles') and fed through the nose until one day an intern asphyxiates her by mistake by pouring her food down the wrong nostril. This is what he desires for her for having spat upon art, 'l'Art pur! sans compter le poète'. In a very literal sense this poem is about the rejection of love and the retention of art, but it is dominated by an image of revenge unspiced with wit and fails to convince.

The 'vingt ans' clue probably means this was a pre-Germany poem though Laforgue may have revised it. Trézenick included it in the issue of *Lutèce* dated 17–24 May 1885.

COMPLAINTE DES CONSOLATIONS

The consolation of sex at street level, which is a consequence one can guess of the situation that occurred in the previous poem, is contrasted to the 'passables' cosmic orgies perceived from the tower of *Notre-Dame*. Below, a chance episode, a chance encounter; above, the observation of other people's chance episodes. Laforgue fails to make an interesting poem from the encounter of poet and prostitute. If, to put it as crudely as Laforgue does, he gets his number in the third stanza 'en m'appliquant bien', and there is little point in the sententiousness of lines like 'D'un *cant* sur le qui-vive au travers de nos hontes!' Indeed, the word 'hontes' seems a lapse, an aberration which reveals a confusion in the poem between the morality of the puzzled bourgeois when he encounters a prostitute and the a-morality of the detached 'decadent' in the same situation. There is no need for either gentleman to be confused about the matter! Consequently, the poem falls flat.

COMPLAINTE DES BONS MENAGES

The 'bon ménage' is with a girlfriend or mistress who is expected to be 'discreet', not disturb the poet's life, be as much part of his décor as the tea-set, and 'fais frou-frou, sans t'inquiéter pourquoi'. She plays her role while he observes it. Because this is such a short and uncomplicated poem, its male condescension is even more flagrant than when the 'chauvinism' is merely a part of a set of emotions deriving from other sorts of situation. The situation here is that the poet amuses himself with a young girl ('laisse-moi bêler tout aux plis de ta jupe') only to decide that other things are more important and that one cannot spend the whole of life in the arms of a woman ('On peut ne pas l'avoir constamment sur les bras!') Consequently it does not matter what girl a man takes up with to pass the time: 'Soyons Lui, Elle et l'Autre'. The poem in fact expresses the same cynical sentiments as Laforgue's letter to Théophile Ysaye just before his marriage: 'Les Corinne, les Ophélie, etc., tout cela, dans notre vie, est mensonge: dans le fond, il n'y a pour nous que les petites Adrienne au bon cœur, aux longs cils, au juvénile et éphémère sourire, les petites Adrienne à la peau enchanteresse, que le hasard (et tout n'est-il pas hasard?) a conduites sur notre chemin. Oui, tout est hasard, car n'eût-il pas existé d'Adrienne, il y aurait eu une Leah; n'y eût-il pas eu de Leah, il y aurait eu une Nini et ainsi de suite' (*OC* v, p. 163). Laforgue was such an inveterate Determinist that he did not mean in this letter to Théophile Ysaye that he was not looking forward to the arrival of Leah Lee, the woman he was to marry. On the contrary, he expresses his impatience as he waits at the little station for her arrival. 'Cette minute me fait palpiter le cœur'. The letter was written while he waited and he imagined the waiting, together with the passage quoted above, *before* he actually went to the station since he takes the letter with him to post on the way. In the same way, 'Complainte des bons Ménages' is an imagined reaction to an event which, if it occurred, did not occur in the manner described. 'J'*aimerais* les plissés de ta colerette'. This means that Laforgue's inveterate determinism is more a manner, a style, a modish way of describing experience, than a deeply felt response to it, which is only another way of saying that 'Complainte des bons Ménages' scarcely plumbs the depth of the human condition. Perhaps Laforgue recognized this when he wrote 'L'Art sans poitrine m'a trop longtemps bercé dupe'. Indeed it had.

COMPLAINTE DE LORD PIERROT
and AUTRE COMPLAINTE DE LORD PIERROT

Laforgue wrote most of the poems for *L'Imitation de Notre-Dame la Lune* after he had completed *Les Complaintes* but there was an overlap. Consequently, these Pierrot poems in *Les Complaintes* may usefully be considered in conjunction with the Pierrot poems in the later volume, that is with 'Pierrots I–V' and 'Locutions de Pierrot'. The adoption of the 'persona' made a difference and the difference was the same in each case. Laforgue had always been interested in the figure of the clown, the uncommitted, passive, perceptive harlequin whose part in the masquerade of life is to be aware that he is playing a part. He himself had grown to like Watteau's painting called *Gilles* in the Louvre where the clown has an air of quiet suffering, of endurance, of affected naïveté and when Stéphane in *Stéphane Vassiliew* made a brief bid to escape from school he went to the circus in the nearby town. Later, Laforgue wrote from Germany about going to circuses. The clown figure suited the Nihilist because of his critical but detached attitude of resignation to circumstance and Laforgue's Pierrot poems are merely one of many contemporary works in which the age-old, traditional imagery of clown and circus is given a rather cynical, joyless rendering consistent with the poet's hostile attitude towards society. Even Ernest Dowson wrote a Pierrot piece, a sure sign that the imagery was a decadent commonplace. The circus clown paintings of Picasso were in the same genre. The adoption of Pierrot by Laforgue as the narrator figure of the poems maybe does not change them very much, because what Pierrot imagines as clown is little different from what Laforgue himself imagines, but the third person singular *seems* to create a different effect, reducing at least slightly the elements of confession and self-pity. Self-pity is only to be expected in a clown. The irony of a clown's confessional can be enjoyed without strain.

The clown or Pierrot figure is also part of the imagery of whiteness. White is the colour of sterility and in Laforgue's poems sets of things are related often only by their whiteness, which is in turn associated with the moon, another image for the negation of the normal. Laforgue's letter to Gustave Kahn, to which G. Jean-Aubry gave a conjectural date of April 1885, states the 'theory' as it were of the Pierrot poems:

Je me suis remballé pour les vers: figure-toi que je veux faire imprimer cet été (mais directment, chez le nommé Trézenick par ex.) une mince plaquette, quelque chose comme *Contribution* (beï-trage) au culte de la lune, plusieurs piècettes à la Lune, un décaméron de pierrots, et sur les succédanés de la lune pendant le jour: les perles, les phtisiques, les cygnes, la neige et les linges. Je t'apporterai ce bouquet et te graverai à la première page une dédicace lapidaire et luminaire. J'ai rattrapé cet enthousiasme d'une paperasse retrouvée où il y avait un tête-à-tête très senti avec la Dame Blanche en question une nuit de juillet dernier, de ma fenêtre, à l'île de la Mainau sur le lac de Constance. (*LA* p. 100)

In the Pierrot poems in *Les Complaintes* these images of the clown and of whiteness, and especially the moon, are made to represent the 'immut-able Unconscious' of Hartmann—the universal law that in Laforgue is invariably imagined in contradistinction to human law. Thus 'Complainte de lord Pierrot' begins:

> Inconscient, descendez en nous par réflexes;
> Brouillez les cartes, les dictionnaires, les sexes.

Apart from the structure given to the poem by this Pierrot theme, 'Complainte de Lord Pierrot' is similar in design to many other poems in the volume. The poet whose heart is at first 'chaste et vrai comme une bonne Lampe' and who cannot distinguish between what he calls human and divine dignity, in the end becomes embittered: 'Bah! j'irai passer la nuit dans le premier train'. He will go anywhere to pass the time, to appease his heart that is now 'triste comme un lampion forain'. This part of the poem is contrasted with the moon dreams of, for example, lines 15–28 where sets of moon and whiteness images amount to 'les menuets de nos pantalonnades'. Once again there is counterpoint between two types of line, two types of verse pattern. Once again the poem is given shape by its beginning and ending with a popular song. Once again there is a type of dialogue, a whimsical dialectic. Both parts, however, relate to the main theme of sexual loneliness and frustration. The frivolity of lines like

> En costume blanc, je ferai le cygne,
> Après nous le Déluge, ô ma Léda!

combines with the Romantic bathos of what, in Laforgue, is almost a refrain—'Ah! qu'une, d'elle-même, un beau soir sût venir',—to make a poem which is really a lament, the lament of a man who has adopted a life 'De moins en moins localisé' and is frustrated.

The agonising of 'Complainte de lord Pierrot' is balanced by the cynical wit of the next poem, 'Autre Complainte de lord Pierrot' (p. 90). There is no Romantic longing in this poem for the woman who will turn up on her own initiative. On the contrary, the masculine-feminine dialogue is terse and biting. The poet luxuriates in the fantasy

that the woman loves him and can therefore be rebuffed. She loves him
absolutely, exclusively: 'tu seras mon seul thème'. For him there are no
absolutes: 'Tout est relatif'. She desires the assurance of fidelity: he
thinks whatever happens is outside human control, is a matter of
chance: 'Autant à qui perd gagne!' She teases him with the lover's
admonition that he will be the first to break off the affair. He replies
with a cold politeness: 'Après vous, s'il vous plaît'. And so on. The
moral is a harsh one. To her who 'doit me mettre au courant de la
Femme', the sum of the angles of a triangle are equal to two right
angles. The eternal couple. The eternal rightness of the couple. For the
poet, apparently, the need to reject this.

COMPLAINTE SUR CERTAINS ENNUIS

A quiet, wistful lyric about a woman who lost a ring and wanted help in
finding it gives rise to a typical Laforgue-type opposition between the
desire for unique experience ('On voudrait s'avouer des choses / ... / Qui
feraient une fois pour toutes!') and the knowledge that everyday life is
trivial and repetitive. The women want to chat or to discuss questions of
social precedence as opposed to the poet, whose thoughts are as usual
serious and introspective. The play in the poem between what the poet
would like and what he has is attractive because understated, yet even
here, in a quite unpretentious poem, it is interesting to note the way in
which Laforgue gives a stanza fibre with lines like 'Par quels gâchis
suresthétiques', where 'gâchis' is a harsh reference to the women's
make-up and textually a harsh sound and shape.

COMPLAINTE DES NOCES DE PIERROT

Pierrot desires a woman who, being a woman, is 'non mortel' but more
like a religious 'pénitente' committed, remotely, to

ces airs plats
Et ces dolentes pantomimes

Pierrot would like to break through the barriers around this 'goddess'
but fails. He says he will be her exorcist, will release her from her role,
but what he desires sounds distinctly like rape. '*Introïbo*', he says,
cheekily. 'Hallali!' Laforgue's hunting word for the sexual chase. This
so-called husband 'songe au pôle' and asks her to guard or save for him
her '*ut* de martyre'. The frankly phallic image and the physiological
innuendo in '*ut*' (musical note but also uterus) are to no avail, however,
since Pierrot fails to consummate his desires: '—Mon dieu! mon dieu!

Je n'ai rien eu'. The woman whom he 'loves' remains aloof and is really just the 'chapel' in which Pierrot from time to time exposes his mood of the moment.

'J'en suis encore aux poncifs thèmes!' A psychoanalytical account might be given of the defensive strategies of this poem. The person of the poem is only Pierrot, whom one would not expect to engage in actual relationships. The woman is a goddess, a remote figure in a chapel fit to be worshipped. The poem consists mostly of a frivolous play upon the conceit that the man who worships may break through the pseudo-religious barriers of the woman who remains aloof. Not much appears to be at stake and the reader cannot legitimately tell whether or not behind the Pierrot mask there is a poet who craves affection and a type of relationship more profound than that posited in the sixth stanza. He cannot tell, but he can guess that, behind the affectation that in the mouth of Pierrot is appropriate, lies an actual desire for the love which this poem negates. Perhaps the poet, destroyed by his own loneliness, had so thoroughly repressed his desires that only the dilettante, defensive pose was possible to him. Therefore, 'J'en suis encore aux poncifs thèmes!'

The word 'frivolous' was used above because the by-play of the first four stanzas and the manipulation of the religious words (dieu, pénitente, pieux, calices, eucharistie...and so on, through the poem) obviously cannot be taken seriously. Whether Laforgue succeeds or not is another matter. He had already used this church language so frequently in the philosophical poems for mock-heroic purposes that to utilize it once more, in this poem, seems questionable, even though the basic strategy of the poem is somewhat different. Perhaps the poem did not belong in the volume at all. The early version had been called 'Complainte de vraie fiancée' but was then extensively revised in proof in 1885. (Debauve reprints the earlier version pp. 165–6.) Conceivably it would have been better for Laforgue at that point to have transferred the poem to *L'Imitation de Notre-Dame la Lune*. If the poem, obliquely, was about a failed engagement it belonged in *Les Complaintes*; if it was a genuine Pierrot poem it belonged in *L'Imitation*.

Reasonably enough some editors have altered the copy-text 's'existe' (l.22) to 'n'existe', treating the grammatically infelicitous first edition reading as a typographical error. Laforgue's pre-occupation with words beginning with the letters 'sex' (e.g. 'sexiproques', 's'exorciser') make it possible that 's'existe' was deliberate.

COMPLAINTE DU VENT QUI S'ENNUIE LA NUIT

If Laforgue showed this kind of poem to R in 1883, or indeed to any other woman, she must have had a reasonably good sense of humour. The wind that is so much a part of Laforgue's imaginative universe keeps the lovers apart so that she has no need to worry about being de-flowered, at least tonight: 'Ta fleur se fane, ô fiancée?' This pretty little idea is sustained through the poem: 'gardes-en...La corolle', 'O calice loyal mais vide', and is in contrast with the wind which on this evening when the poet is forced to resort to his books ('Un soir d'ennui trop studieux!') represents the raging of unfulfilled passion. In a ship-wreck which was 'nostalgic' because the present when he is by himself is so different from the past when they were together, he was thrown her golden fleece, so that being stranded was bearable; but now love is in a state of siege. The refrain is highly elliptical and seems to mean that while love is under siege he who would commit the 'sacrilege' of filling her 'calice loyal' if he could reach her is in fact 'pris au piège', that is, he, too, is stuck where he is and, like an animal in a snare, 'Geint sans retour'. The conclusion is neat. The ravaged intellectual air of the green curtains of their vault (the room in which they customarily meet) and the banal marble of the bathroom constitute the image, the very reflection of his tomb. He is dead without her! Bedroom and bathroom are his tomb! Who else in 1885 would have the impudence to rhyme 'hypogée' with 'ravagée' or 'tombeau', that venerable classic, with 'lavabo'? And who else would have perpetrated the ghastly adjectival pun on 'hypogée', abstruse word whose obscure double meaning the Littré reveals? Finally, perhaps the frustrated love that was whimpering in its snare will be killed before the night is over. The discourse of the wind this stormy night amounts to no more than

> Des vains cortèges
> De l'humour

COMPLAINTES DU PAUVRE CORPS HUMAIN

In its very simplicity this poem demonstrates the extent to which Laforgue had parted company with the traditional nineteenth-century poet. To write a poem about the body, without attributing to it any type of spiritual or metaphysical significance, might now seem a quite ordinary thing to do. Not so in 1885. Even to imagine the body in purely physical terms was a bold and radical step, here compounded by Laforgue's cynicism. Far from being the temple of the Lord, the poet's body is imagined as being separate from the poet who observes and thinks about it. It has a covering of nerve ends, like a coat of mail which protects it from 'Un fier répertoire d'attaques'. Within, it is 'un cloaque', a sink which gathers the refuse of existence. This body may be smartly dressed on Sundays, having sweated all week at work, but if seen naked in bed, 'Dans un décor d'oiseaux, de roses', it is revealed as capable of reflex action only, of 'tics réflexes' and 'mondaines poses'. Lying back on a green bed, is the implication, the body is not the romantic beauty celebrated by lovers but a sort of disaster of the nervous system: 'sa chlorose'. Virtue and sensuality inhabit this body only to war over its possession. It cares for itself, drugs, shears, perfumes, decks itself out, only to die later. And when it dies it decays,

> Et la cuisine se résume
> En mille infections posthumes.

In other words, the body does not even have to be alive to be itself. Death is merely a stage in the process of decay, not a moment which is important because of loss of consciousness. Look at this couple who make so much of their bodies, the poet exclaims cynically. Really, nature is 'sans pitié'. What the body does is purely, merely physical and germs of conscience are 'fols'. When one considers not only the high-toned concepts that religious people still associate with the human body and the guilt that is still felt by many simply over its functions, one can appreciate the novelty of this poem for 1885. A line like 'Ces fols germes de conscience' would not merely be offensive to a middle-class reader brought up to believe that there were rules of behaviour on which civilization depended. It might very well be incomprehensible and therefore inherently dangerous. This is all the more the case, given the poem's lightness of touch. Laforgue succeeds in guiding the reader through the poem by means of minor variations in the two line refrain, so that attention is drawn, variously, to the man, to the woman, to the couple. This works. The heavy 'attack' of some of the other poems is here avoided and the result is a cuttingly ironic poem on a subject many of Laforgue's readers would have regarded as a sacrosanct.

COMPLAINTE DU ROI DE THULE

Thule is the remote, cold, impersonal northern land where nothing grows and where life, in the sense of procreation, breeding, sex, is denied. The King of Thule was immaculate, a virgin not involved in sex, 'loin des jupes et des choses'. The Sun, by contrast, was worn out by the effort of presiding daily over the 'mammalian orgies' of the cult called Love. No wonder he, the sun, bleeds to death or near death at the end of each day, 'devant la nuit fauve'. To compensate for this the King, usually occupied with laments over the metamorphosis of lilies into roses, of the pure into the passionate, the white into the bloody, makes for the Sun

> ...un certain Voile
> de vive toile,

(veil, sail, winding cloth) and rows across the waters so that he can tend for the sun. The pure love of the King of Thule transcends the sexual love of which the Sun was progenitor and thus casts a shade over young lovers who should keep him out ('Tournez vos clés') if they desire to enjoy their nights together ('Brave amants! aux nuits de lait').

Presumably this poem is so frequently chosen as the anthology piece to represent *Les Complaintes* because it is not doctrinaire, because it has the lightness of touch of the best of the 'Complaintes' with the little speech at the centre enclosed by stanzas in a different form, because of the dramatic realization in the 'characters' of the Sun and the King of Thule which precludes those nakedly autobiographical elements in some of the other poems, and because there is a pleasing ambivalence in the 'action' which derives partly from the word 'voile' itself, and partly from enigmatic features like the play upon the difference between the King 'traînant des clés' and the lovers who must turn their keys to keep out the King if they wish to believe in love. It is indeed an excellent anthology piece though readers familiar with the volume as a whole may decide that it is not representative.

COMPLAINTE DU SOIR DES COMICES AGRICOLES

Mentioned first in Laforgue's letter to Gustave Kahn dated, by G. Jean-Aubry, February 1884, this poem like so many others was revised in 1885.

> Et voilà, comme disait en signant Boquillon dans sa *Lanterne* qu'au lycée, en province, nous lisions tous les dimanches. Maintenant, pour goûter cette chose, il faudrait chanter les refrains sur un air de cors de chasse que j'ai entendu dans mon enfance en province, des piqueurs qui l'après-midi parcouraient la ville, portant en étendard le programme du cirque anglo-americain, et aussi écrire le mot mystère en lettres gothiques ou mieux en lettres onciales.

With these words Laforgue introduced the poem to his friend, showing as he did so that the images of the hunting horn, the agricultural fair, the circus were deeply imbedded in his imagination as symbols of the traditional life which went on for century after century and from which he dissociated himself. Despite the dissociation, however, there is also nostalgia. 'Loin du bal', that is far away from the festivity that gives rise to the poem, is the recollection of more primitive country celebrations. Shall the poet remember them with affection or will he place them in the *fin-de-siècle* tradition that derived from the agricultural fair in *Madame Bovary*? The violin that is 'incompris' because it generates enigmatic and tender memories of his native country and the mechanical organ that brings him to the brink of 'un appel vers l'Idéal' are both part of a reverie that modifies Laforgue's habitual harshness.

After the hunt, the wedding. The sexual metaphors of the hunting horns and the hunters' rifles give way to that of the dance which, for one night, this agricultural community enjoys. The hunt was an inevitable part of existence; so is the coupling of man and woman in dance, sex, marriage. For these 'gens de la noce', though, the hunting is over because to couple or to be a couple is 'le sort de la race'. There is no explanation for this: 'Tout est un triste et vieux Mystère'. You might as well drink and dance through the evening, therefore, while the young couple wanders in the fields 'parmi les rêves des grillons'.

Given the fact of Laforgue's pessimism, this poem is one of the more deft and successful treatments of what, for him, was a common theme: the foolishness of celebration and particularly sexual or matrimonial celebration.

It is interesting to note the way in which Laforgue forces his own meanings on to an experience which obviously could be imagined in so many different ways. An agricultural fair or feast day gives rise to the all encompassing comment:

...ô race humaine,
Vous me faites bien de la peine.

This persistent pessimism in Laforgue shows in the changes he made to the version he sent to Kahn. The length and structure of the poem remained basically the same in the first edition text, but there were a number of emendations. 'Se recrotter' in l. 8 had previously been 'se resalir'; 'ce besoin insensé' in l. 26 had previously been 'le diabolique accès'. (Conceivably Laforgue had been persuaded away from the unsubtle sexual word 'accès'.) Line 23 had previously read 'Geignent les cruautés dont le spleen est témoin'. The idea that 'spleen' is in some way a witness to the 'cruelty' of sex which is itself a type of 'complaint' is as unsubtle as 'accès'. The greatly overworked word 'spleen' did little for the poem. The new line 23 was harsher, more ironical, more bitter, more in the spirit of the poem, less abstract. The couple who walked out over the fields away from the crowd, away from the music, act out 'Dans les foins' the ancient 'mystery' of sex from which encounter burst out two fledgling dreams, 'sans maire et sans adjoint', that is, without authority to make the union legitimate and without witness to give it validity.

That Laforgue re-wrote this line in this way in one sense substantiates the notion that he did in fact force his meanings upon experience. Enough is said in the poem to make the reader feel it had an occasion. The poet witnessed the scene, the festivity, the dancing, the young couple walking away into the fields: 'le spleen est témoin'. If that was the case, he (not the scene observed) generated the comments that make up much of the poem. This fact alone governs the reactions of those readers who are repelled by Laforgue's cynicism, in that his interpretation of common experience, of the most ordinary and simple things like making love, stems from sets of attitudes which have been previously established in his mind and which are rarely justified in the poem itself. Such readers may not be convinced by the stock argument of many literature departments viz. that to say Laforgue 'forced a meaning on experience' is not a literary comment at all, that the poem ought to be accepted for what it is, and that what it is rests in its language and in its cynical wit, in short that it is a made poem and not one which in any true sense describes experiences, whether the poet's or anybody else's. This line of thought, however, only leads to the conclusion that the boundary lines around the merely verbal are difficult to define. Is it possible to write witty, detached, intellectual poems that will exist solely within the verbal idiom of the poet's ideas, responses, attitudes or will there always be teasing 'references', however oblique, to the world in which the rest of us live? 'Complainte du Soir des Comices Agricoles', in many ways such a successful poem, perhaps demonstrates how difficult it is to be completely detached without slipping into tawdry and questionable subjective attitudinizing.

COMPLAINTE DES CLOCHES

This squib was written in August 1883 in Liège and takes its rightful place, as it were, in the centre of the volume as a poem whose sounds are analogous to real life sounds, in this instance bells.

It needed no more than the church bells on Sunday morning to trigger off sets of verses like these, in which Laforgue's atheism, cynicism, pessimism could be re-asserted in impudent ironies and inversions, the simple contrast between what the bells were supposed to represent and what life was actually like being enough to make the poem. The poem is the chant of the black satyrs of an anti-Christ and its conclusion is: 'Nous retombe à jamais BÊTE'. His anti-religious imagery obviously dates his poems to a period in which the religious and the bourgeois were close to being the same thing. Attack one and you attack the other. The events of the twentieth century have made this type of sprightly iconoclasm almost impossible. Laforgue would have realized this and, one hopes, would have deleted from subsequent editions of *Les Complaintes* the pathetic footnote at the end of 'Complainte des Cloches', by which he attempted to generalize its impudence. Coinages like 'Hymniclames!' are not inappropriate in a lively little squib: in a poem which affected a greater seriousness it would be hard to endure.

COMPLAINTES DES GRANDS PINS
DANS UNE VILLA ABANDONEE

A quite straightforward poem in the, by this time, familiar contrapuntal or Impressionist style of the main group of poems, 'Complainte des grands Pins dans une Villa abandonnée' was conceived and perhaps written in 1882, for the notations in Marie Laforgue's copy read: 'Octobre 1882, boulevard Saint-Michel'. This would mean that he wrote it in his Paris hotel, 'fade chambre', while breaking his return journey from Tarbes to Germany at the end of his summer vacation. In a letter to his sister, he referred to the dismal weather that the poem also describes: 'Depuis trois jours, averses torrentielles et inépuisables, je rentre trempé'. (Perhaps this coincided with the beginning of the long series of illnesses that eventually resulted in the complete breakdown of his health.) Laforgue must have revised this poem, however, the following spring when the idea of a volume of 'Complaintes' took hold. The poem is marked 'A Bade' and it is mentioned in the 20 May entry in the *Agenda* for 1883.

The occasion of the writing of the poem is mentioned because the poem fails to transcend the occasional. Its details seem unworked, are left on the level of mere recollection. What is the 'villa abandonnée' of the title? What is the role in the poem of 'Berthe aux sages yeux de lilas'? Why, when he dies, will he be sent to Montmartre,

> Loin de père et mère, enterrés
> En Alsace.

Who were these women, 'coudes nus dans les fruits' who caused him such agony? And in what circumstance did those servants make 'piles' of money at his expense? These superficially anecdotal elements may be linked by association in the poet's mind but they are not linked by association in the poem. Consequently they distract the reader away from the poem along unwarranted lines of speculation. This failure only serves to emphasise the anonymous, impersonal nature of Impressionist art. Here we have piecemeal, fragmented 'impressions' of experience, but since they are anecdotal by nature they resist the poet's attempt to make them into a poem.

COMPLAINTE SUR CERTAINS TEMPS DEPLACES

The great Mystery this poem celebrates is the poet's awareness of his private, internal existence which, though at odds with, is independent of the external world. As for the real (i.e. physical) world—'Mais jugez si ça m'importune'. Life in this sense is for 'les badauds', for people who wish to observe and chat about it superficially. By contrast, the poet dreams of an imaginative world, his Venice, which is protected from the elements, the storms and winds of this poem, and which is a refuge also from the triviality of hoping for 'adventure' in the little world that, by comparison with Nature, is no bigger than a ring-railway: 'Le chemin d'fer Paris-Ceinture'.

Let us see how this poem works. It is a 'Complainte sur certains temps déplacés'. The poet is displaced. The poem reflects the dislocation. Not only is it reflected, it also exists in the structural breaks of the poem itself. The stanzas do not constitute a logical sequence but are impressionistic strokes which only make sense when the inexplicit associations between them are accepted as a totality, that is as an imaginative not a logical totality. Thus the dislocation permits a distinctive type of creation, one in which verbal formulations are exactly equated not with things themselves but with the poet's response to them. In this poem, there are hints enough of an actual occasion: '—V'la le fontainier!' makes it seem that a scene is being observed. The immediacy of the sunset gives this impression as well, which is reinforced by the personal pronoun. The present tense quality of the poem cannot be doubted: in that sense it is immediate. On the other hand, the poem obviously is not descriptive: the references to a scene are only one part of the complex of responses that make the poem and these references are outweighed by the poem's metaphors. The sunset is stained with blood like a butcher's bench. The poet, too, might be skinned and butchered by whoever caused the death of the sun. But he lives, not dies, in the aura of the sun, 'comme un poitrail de chambellan' so that when the sun dies he is 'displaced'. The reader is forced to search out the connections of metaphor without the help of any connections of logic, so that there is a consistency between the fragmented experience of 'le cœur tout nomade' and the associated verbal or metaphorical fragments of the poem. The hint of sexual metaphor is, for example, left in the poem as an implication, an element that this time is not explored. 'Passez, ô nuptials appels' is whimsically linked with 'Paris-Ceinture', but the poet will be without adventure, without sex, alone in his room that overlooks the sea where bitterness, his spleen, rises as he spells out the gross mystery of existence 'en stylite'. The conciseness and economy of the poem, together with the originality of its language, is thus counter-balanced by enigmatic internal relationships which never completely reveal their whole meaning. In general, this technique works, as it probably does here, if there genuinely is originality of language and metaphor, whereas it tends to fail when Laforgue is uncertain in his touch or resorts to his basic stockpile of Nihilist metaphor.

This was one of the poems taken by Trézenick for the magazine *Lutèce*, where it appeared in the issue dated 21–8 June 1885.

COMPLAINTES DES CONDOLEANCES AU SOLEIL

Taken by Trézenick for *Lutèce* (21–8 June 1885), perhaps revised in 1885 but written in 1881 before Laforgue went to Germany, this poem was one of those smuggled in by Laforgue to make up the collection. Its heavy phrasing links it immediately to poems like 'Complainte du Sage de Paris' and 'Préludes Autobiographiques' and places it in that group of poems anticipated in the 'Preamble', the group for which detailed exegesis except with the dictionary at hand would be quite pointless. In fact it is difficult to know why Laforgue wished to include such a poem, given the subtlety or deftness of many of the others.

COMPLAINTE DE L'OUBLI DES MORTS

A light, song-like poem which, despite its ominous undertone, does not need comment or explanation. The varied stanza and the tension between the seriousness of the subject and the lightly cynical tone make it a typical 'Complainte'. Its position in the volume does a little to distract the attention from the dreary over-seriousness of the poem which precedes it.

COMPLAINTE DU PAUVRE JEUNE HOMME

Another lighter poem, the unwary reader thinks to himself, but, alas, another footnote too! One cannot tell with absolute certainty that the footnote was Laforgue's doing but, since its effect alters the meaning of the line, l. 41, completely, it can only be regretted. That the husband might commit suicide when his wife left him makes a kind of sense but not if he will not speak 'un mot de blâme'. In other respects the poem is a successful rendering of a little theme to the rhythm of a popular tune. In fact it is almost like a ballad and in this *genre* is one of Laforgue's better poems.

COMPLAINTE DE L'EPOUX OUTRAGE

This ballad type dialogue between the husband and wife who has been unfaithful to him was almost certainly written in 1883, when the idea of writing poems to the tunes of popular songs seized Laforgue.

COMPLAINTE-VARIATIONS SUR LE MOT 'FALOT, FALOTTE'

Here is another light-spirited poem written to the infectiously insistent rhythm of a song or perhaps to the rhythm of a train as it travels across the countryside. Metaphysical anguish is not the dominant feature of the poem for once, although Laforgue was unable to resist the last stanza which, except in the context of the volume as a whole, has little to do with this poem. More precisely, the various stanzas, each of which constitutes a little cameo or picture, are indeed like circles in the water of the poet's imagination, but 'les beaux lacs de l'Idéal' are something of an imposition coming, as they do, after a series of sharply visualized vignettes.

COMPLAINTE DU TEMPS ET DE SA COMMERE L'ESPACE

The preceding poem, 'sur le mot "falot, falotte" ', brought to an end the central section of *Les Complaintes*, which for the most part consisted of poems written in 1883 or 1884. The volume would have been roughly a hundred pages long without the additon of the early poems to which we return with 'Complainte du Temps et de sa Commère l'Espace'. Perhaps in 1885 Laforgue had genuinely forgotten the lighthearted mood which had inspired the writing of the 'Complaintes' during his friendship with R in the spring of 1883. Or perhaps, on reflection, he decided that to have only the non-'philosophical' poems would seriously misrepresent him. It will be obvious that the present editor regrets Laforgue's decision. Yet each reader will naturally arrive at his own judgement of the matter.

Any reader who has persevered with either the poems or the commentaries to this point will recognize that, in Laforgue's dialogue between himself and the Unconscious Will, the answers to his questions 'Mais quel fut mon but? Je t'ai, tu m'as. Mais où?' consist of ideas from Hartmann, not on this occasion 'bathed in dream' or spiced with 'une mélancolie humoristique'.

GRANDE COMPLAINTE DE LA VILLE DE PARIS

An Impressionistic, prose poem, 'Grande Complainte de la Ville de Paris' anticipates the flimsy prose sketches that make up 'Chroniques Parisiennes' in its almost exclusive interest in surface detail. The technique is to discover interesting or 'different' words for the visible and, for the most part, quite ordinary aspects of the Paris scene. In that the visual details and the verbal formulations of phrases constitute a quite arbitrary mosaic constructed from ephemeral aspects of city existence, this prose poem directly resembles some types of Impressionist painting, as do some of the other poems in the collection. As such, it has a certain panache. On the other hand, it is doubtful whether it really fits into the volume and it is doubtful whether Laforgue had the ability to write an imaginatively coherent prose sketch. Furthermore, the force of the word 'élite' is difficult to estimate. Laforgue refers to 'l'inextirpable élite' and at the end of the same paragraph says 'Que les vingt-quatre heures vont vite à la discrète élite'. This seems an odd *volte-face*. Many of the poems in the volume are fundamentally elitist in their point of view, or in the implications of their point of view, whereas this poem comes close to adopting a modish, anarchic stance, as though the attitudes that could be maintained in the seclusion of a foreign palace were being dropped by the poet in his Paris hotel room. One searches for an explanation when it may be simply that the poet was in a bad mood when he began the poem in rue Madame in 1884.

COMPLAINTE DES MOUNIS DU MONT-MARTRE

The earlier version of this poem was published in the October 1892 issue of *EPL*. The language (with coinages like the wildly absurd 'S'in-Pan-filtre') and the ideas (e.g. the post-Darwinian image of insects, men, thoughts being ephemera which live briefly in the evening sun and die) indicate an early poem. On the other hand, the impressionistic, non-sequential form of the poem is a sure sign that it was written or re-written after 1883, as is the turn of thought of lines 34–8, for example, where the chronometer image from the beginnning of the poem, the idea of life slipping away in fragments inexorably, is transferred to the movement of the jaw as man eats his way through his existence—'au gâteau du Temps'. The poem is a 'Complainte des Mounis' because a Buddhist type of resignation is needed when the meaning of existence cannot be determined and when everything seems ephemeral: 'Vous n'avez point cure/De ce que peut être cette aventure.' Laforgue failed to escape from the late nineteenth-century depression that derived from the non-Christian, post-Darwinian cosmology that, for instance, Wallace Stevens was later to celebrate in the poem *Sunday Morning* (*Collected Poems*, Alfred Knopf, 1955). 'We live in an old chaos of the sun', said Stevens, meaning that man's earth was only one of thousands and that life on it was accidental or, as he says, 'casual'. In this poem of Laforgue's the suns, the heavenly bodies, are weeded out of the universe 'à jamais' (i.e. as part of a continuous process) and existence occurs in brief indeterminate intervals of time ('O laps sans digues'). Time is therefore incomprehensible. This being the case, why does Time not stop fooling about: 'Et cesser ce jeu!' Why would not time consider what he is doing—'Lui mettre le nez dans son Œuvre'. Laforgue in this poem simply allows himself to sport with a set of notions and metaphors that were commonplaces of his imagination.

COMPLAINTE-LITANIES DE MON SACRE-CŒUR

Laforgue's revision of 'Litanies de mon Sacré-Cœur' in 1885 cannot have been extensive. It had originally been written in 1881 and bears many of the marks of a poem written before Laforgue went to Germany; the unexciting twelve syllable line, the inversion of a religious idea (this is the litany of an atheist who desires human not heavenly love) and the extravagance of phrasing without the alleviation of wit as in expressions like 'De ce vin revomi, l'universel dégoût'. Though it contains stock ideas and could be related thematically to other poems in the volume, by Laforgue's standards of inventiveness it is little more than a piecemeal exercise in rhyme making. He sent it to Vanier for the first time in April 1885 and Trézenick put it into the 19–23 June number of *Lutèce*.

COMPLAINTE DES DEBATS MELANCOLIQUES ET LITTERAIRES

Almost certainly an early poem, this too was sent to Vanier in April 1885 as part of Laforgue's attempt to make up the volume to fifty poems. What Laforgue thought about himself in his early days is here expressed simply enough: 'Le cœur me piaffe de génie / Eperdument pourtant...' Certainly there is a mild irony in 'piaffe', as indeed the poem as a whole has an air of bravado about it, but basically Laforgue felt himself unjustly not known and unjustly not loved. In the context of the volume, the last six lines that disturb the artifice by an apparent particularity of reference are surely a lapse. The introduction of this anecdotal element, the named person Helen making tea downstairs while the poet shivers by himself upstairs, though consistent with the vein of self-pity that runs through the poem, is nonetheless on a more fundamental level inconsistent. In any case, the reader does not know where he stands, since too little information is given for him to understand the relation between the last six lines and the poem which precedes them.

COMPLAINTE D'UNE CONVALESCENCE EN MAI

This brilliant poem was a late addition to the volume. Written in Coblenz between 6–29 November 1884 and at first called simply 'Convalescence', the first known draft was included as part of a letter to Gustave Kahn in Paris. Pia suggests that this manuscript was the missing part of *LA* XIX, dated March 1885 by G. Jean-Aubry, and reprints this first, twenty-eight line version verbatim from a sale catalogue. Since there are few opportunities to see Laforgue at work, as it were, the early version is reproduced here as well:

> Convalescence au lit, ancré de courbatures,
> Je m'égare aux dessins bleus de ma couverture.
>
> Las de reconstituer dans l'art du jour baissant
> Cette dame d'en face auscultant les passants.
>
> (Si la mort de son van avait chosé mon être,
> En serait-elle moins ce soir à sa fenêtre?)
>
> Ah! que de soirs de mai pareils à celui-ci!
> Que la vie est égale et le cœur endurci!

Je me sens fou d'un tas de petites misères!
Mais maintenant je sais ce qu'il me reste à faire.

Qui n'a jamais rêvé? Je voudrais le savoir!
Elle[s] vous sourient avec âme, et puis bonsoir,

Ni vu, ni connu! Et les voilà qui rebrodent
L'ingénu canevas de leur âme à la mode,

Fraîches à tous, et puis réservant leur air sec
Pour les Christs déclassés et autres gens suspects!

N'est-ce pas que je sais ce qu'il me reste à faire,
Mon cœur mort pétri d'aromates littéraires,

Et toi cerveau confit dans l'alcool de l'orgeuil
Et qu'il faut procéder d'abord par demi-deuils?

Primo: mes grandes angoisses métaphysiques
Sont passées à l'état de chagrins domestiques.

Deux ou trois spleens locaux...Ah! pitié! voyager
Du moins, pendant un an ou deux à l'étranger!

Plonger mon front dans l'eau des mers, aux matinées
Torrides; m'en aller à petites journées...

—Voici l'œuf à la coque et la lampe du soir.
—Convalescence bien folle! comme on peut voir;

On the same manuscript leaf as the poem, Laforgue wrote: 'A la dernière heure je t'envoie des vers: tout frais de mise au net, mais thème de Paris, d'antan.' By 'theme' Laforgue meant the anguish of loving someone and not being loved in return, an emotion which had mingled painfully with others while he was ill in Coblenz. 'Convalescence' meant recovery, not just literally from a near fatal illness, but also from the pain of being scorned by people to whom he had opened his heart. 'Figure-toi', he said to Henry, 'que j'ai été malade tout ce temps-çi: palpitations, point de côté etc., et absolument veule' (*OC* v, p. 103). This was the physical illness. But the real illness and the recollection of disagreeable experiences in Paris both gave way to the poem as Laforgue fashioned or re-fashioned it in the spring of 1885, adding what are now stanzas 4, 5, 11, 12, 18 and 19, as well as the epigraph, and making a number of other changes, one of which, incidentally, the replacement of 'chant-huant' by 'chat-huant', was not printed in the first edition. This last detail, together with the fact that the proof title was simply 'Complainte d'une Convalescence', seems to confirm that the poem was a late addition to the volume and was not at first conceived as a 'Complainte'.

Claude Pichois has pointed out that the loose quotation from Mme Perier's life of her brother, which Laforgue inserted as an epigraph, came from the passage which described the barbed iron belt which he wore under his clothes: 'Mais tout cela était si secret que nous n'en savions rien du tout, et nous ne l'avons appris qu'après sa mort d'une personne de très grande vertu qu'il aimait et à qui il avait été obligé de le dire pour les raisons qui la regardaient elle-même.' Laforgue's penitential iron belt was the memory of humiliating rejections: his secret the overwhelming seriousness of his 'grandes angoisses métaphysiques'—as he supposed. Charactistically, these sentiments are transformed in the poem into bitter, ironic oppositions. The man's dead heart is preserved in literary spices and the woman's brain in an alcoholic confection of pride. The poem's many brilliantly aphoristic lines compensate, perhaps over-compensate, for the underlying element of self-pity—an element expressed somewhat nakedly in the first version but transmuted in the second by lines like 'Et voilà que mon Ame est tout hallucinée!' and by additional couplets like the penultimate one, where the autobiographical implications of a poem written in the first person are distanced by metaphor.

This is another poem which illustrates the difficulties experienced in 1885 by publisher and printer. In learning to accept the extraordinary liberties Laforgue took, for example in l. 5 where he invents a verb from the noun 'chose' meaning literally 'make into a thing', Vanier and Trézenick inevitably made mistakes of transcription. In the case of this particular poem, Laforgue's letter to Kahn probably provides a clue to the unreliability of the first edition text as printed. Both ll. 12 and 15 of the early version seem preferable to the first edition text. The 'Qui n'a jamais rêvé?' for example, where the 'm'a' of the first edition text is of course a misprint missed in proof, gives the poem a wider reference than it seems at first to have: despite the facts of illness, death, personal misunderstanding, bitterness, loneliness, who has not dreamt that the happiness of May evenings might not endure? To spot possible errors of transcription in this way suggests that there may be others more difficult to identify.

There is a letter from Laforgue to Henry which shows that Laforgue attempted to sustain his friendship with R when she moved to Paris but that he was repulsed. An experience of this kind seems to be behind the poem. Its spirit is a despairing one comparable to that in T. S. Eliot's line: 'I have measured out my life in coffee spoons'. For Laforgue 'mes grandes angoisses métaphysiques / Sont passées à l'état de chagrins domestiques'. This is the lament of the man who is not Prince Hamlet, nor was meant to be: a modern man whose two or three 'spleens locaux' may be without significance in the great scheme of things, and whose restricted hammock life of convalescence allows him only to dream of the Ganges, the symbol of the infinite from which this actual poet is cut off, for he is only capable of little walks in the sunlight amongst the whitewashed houses of the town and of little thoughts: 'Je me sens fou d'un tas de petites misères'. Such a man, goes the lament of the poem, cannot expect to be loved, for fashionable women 'qui rebrodent / Le canevas ingrat de leur âme à la mode', will necessarily despise him and be ungrateful, that is not reciprocate his generous feelings, '...reprenant leur air sec / Pour les christs déclassés et autres gens suspects'. Someone who does not fit into the social scheme of things, who cannot be associated with a certain class, with a certain family, and who is socially 'suspect' despite the fact of his 'bon cœur étant connu', is indeed in bourgeois or capitalist words 'un christ déclassé', an outcast, a misfit, a person who suffers without anyone caring whether he suffers or not.

This poem is not overstated and if it succeeds it does so because the balance between the personal and the general, the psychological and the metaphysical, is maintained by means of a controlled, not a strident irony.

COMPLAINTE DU SAGE DE PARIS

Extended comment on this poem would be superfluous, since it is merely a restatement of the Hartmann-esque ideas which inform the whole volume. As mentioned earlier, it was originally included to balance 'Préludes Autobiographiques' so that the volume would have a 'Sanglot' type poem at the beginning and at the end. When other early poems were added, it held its place. That it is an early poem is sufficiently indicated both by its alexandrine couplets whose mobile caesura creates, despite its mobility, fairly conventional sounds and by its not too unconventional rhymes.

Anyone who has read this far will readily recognize the cluster of ideas that made up the world of the Unconscious; 'les rites réciproques' of any couple that has to cope, somehow, in a senseless but sexual dream world; 'ces claviers anonymes'—the human instrument on which fate plays, here analysed (but without hope) for the sake of art; the bed that is associated simultaneously with sex and death—'Cancans, et fadeur d'hôpital du même lit'; 'les arts enfantins'—childish, because mankind merely uses them as toys to while away the time; the determinism—'Tout est écrit et vrai'; the contrast between people who merely function unthinkingly, who 'rhyme' with the Unconscious, and those who are conscious and therefore painfully detached; 'le Gange'—forever in Laforgue the symbol of the impersonal fact of fate; the image of 'les bas-fonds sous-marins', with 'Les polypes sournois attendant l'hameçon', an image which is made to represent the psychological necessities of instinct and conditioned response; the post-Darwinian, negatively interpreted strain of ideas—'nous nous aimerions / A la grâce des divines sélections'; the outsider, the Levite, who 'sur des oreillers d'étiquettes d'éthetiques' creates 'ronrons lyriques' without reflection, without pausing to consider how uncertain he necessarily is about his own predicament. 'Tout est si compliqué'. Indeed. As in other poems, Laforgue associates this strange world of negatives, this world of experiences which are never to be trusted but are always the consequence of a mysterious Process that must exist but is outside man's comprehension, with something else that is outside his comprehension, the failure of love, the rejection of one person by another, which Laforgue handles here with bitterness, even anger:

> Allons, tu m'as compris. Va, que ta seule étude
> Soit de vivre sans but, fou de mansuétude.

In short, the poem repeats a familiar Laforgue equation. Man desires a faith. Faith is denied by the nature of existence. Man desires love. Love is denied by the nature of existence—or, could it be? by a woman who declines to understand that, behind Laforgue's negative attitudes, there is concealed a warm heart! The two types of denial are inextricably associated in Laforgue's imagination. His better poems are ones in which this equation is located in an imaginative experience with which the reader can identify. The less successful ones are poems in which the ideas are stated baldly as ideas. 'Complainte du Sage de Paris' is in the less successful category.

COMPLAINTE DES COMPLAINTES

A possible first reaction to 'Complainte des Complaintes' is that the volume will not be helped by apologia. It has either, on balance, succeeded or it has not. Why then must Laforgue ask us not to ignore 'les fugues vraies / Que crie, au fond, ma riche voix'? Juggling once again with the concepts of art and faith, or recollecting with self-pity 'un défunt Moi' will not help us very much, we at first think. The volume must justify itself. Yet once again the reader is captivated by the poem which leads him neatly along such a familiar path to the last stanza—a stanza whose wry humour is not overstated but indeed is almost epigrammatic in its economy.

Towards the capstan of our incurable habit of questioning (such seems the import of Laforgue's construction), we make vain fantasies of belief into our own music, never giving up. In this sense we are 'Sisyphes par persuasion'—that is, bound to lose but inevitably continuing the struggle to find solutions to the 'pourquoi' through art. But on this earth, the earth on which we just happened to be, 'ô Terre d'occasion', the religious goals, the beliefs towards which we strive are 'mirages'.

NOTES

INTRODUCTION

1. *MP*, pp. 7–8.
2. Cf. *MP*, p. 11.
3. In a letter to Max Klinger written in 1883, probably in June (*OC* v, 30), Laforgue said: 'Vous arriverez trop tard pour voir le Salon, et, qui est plus irréparable, l'exposition de Sisley.' The technique adopted by Monet and Sisley of breaking down the subject, as it were, into sets of effects observable in a certain light and in certain conditions was analogous to Laforgue's technique of verse fracture. For this reason, it is interesting to note his appreciation of Sisley.
4. *OC* iv, p. 42. Anyone interested in pursuing this should look up Ephrussi's reviews of the 5th and 6th 'Exposition des Artistes Indépendants' in *GBA*. Ephrussi was particularly fond of Berthe Morisot. Note also that passages of this kind give a clue to the fact that, when Laforgue seems to be describing landscape in *Les Complaintes*, he may be referring to paintings, e.g. those many Impressionist paintings of poppy fields.
5. *MP*, p. 183. See Albert Boime's excellent book on the influence and history of the Salon and the Academy, *The Academy and French Paintings in the Nineteenth Century*, Phaidon, 1971.
6. David Arkell's note to me on this subject reads as follows: 'In the catalogue of a Monet exhibition at the Lefèvre Gallery (London) in May 69 Denys Sutton wrote: "In his perceptive essay on Impressionism, the poet Jules Laforgue noted that the Impressionist artist is one who 'sees and depicts nature just as it is, that is uniquely with coloured vibrations'. This response to the interplay of vibrations gives Monet's paintings of La Grenouillère their special character." I'm sure this juxtaposition of Laf and La Grenouillère is no accident. For me it is the key picture about which he is thinking throughout the essay and indeed at many other times too. "Notre Monet" he called it on *OC* iv, 117. And "que tramez-vous entre votre Grenouillère de Monet et le Constantin Guys de Manet?" on *OC* iv, 88. And (on *OC* iv, 30) "Mes amitiès au Claude Monet que vous savez." '
7. Pissarro's brother was a close friend of Laforgue's father. See *LA*, p. 27.
8. I owe this information about the Bernstein's paintings to David

Arkell, who notes also that they possessed one of Monet's 'Champs de Coquelicots'.

9. Note, for example, *LA*, p. 114: 'Tu vas voir des Claude Monet? C'est assurément le plus *calé*, le plus égal (non le plus aigu, etc.) des impressionnistes.' This letter was probably written in 1885. Laforgue had to bring his friend, who had been away, up to date.

10. 'J'écris un article sur l'Impressionnisme, article qui sera traduit et paraîtra dans une revue allemande, à l'occasion de quoi un ami de Berlin, qui a une dizaine d'impressionnistes, en fera une exposition.' *OC* v, p. 7.

11. *OC* v, p. 60.

12. Reprinted in Emile Zola, *Monet. Salon. Manet. Ecrits sur l'Art*, ed. A. Ehrard, Paris, Garnier-Flammarion, 1970.

13. Reprinted in J. K. Huysmans, 'Le Salon de 1879' in *Œuvres completes de J. K. Huysmans*, Vol. vi, *L'Art Moderne*, Paris, Editions Crès, 1929. Laforgue presented a copy of *Les Complaintes* to Huysmans.

14. 'Exposition des Artistes Indépendants' *GBA*, i, 1880, pp. 485–8.

15. ibid, pp. 485–6.

16. Mp. p. 66.

17. *RB*, 7e année, T.x, No. 67, 15 Mars 1896.

18. In the Commentaries which follow the text in this edition, there is an attempt to demonstrate that not all the poems Laforgue chose to include are 'Complaintes' in the strict sense. The analogy between Laforgue's ideas about Impressionism and his own work applies most completely to the poems written in 1883.

19. 'Notes d'esthétique', *RB*, 7 année, T.x, No. 84, 1 Dec. 1896. Part of this was reprinted in *MP*, p. 152.

20. *MP*, p. 136.

21. Reprinted in Debauve, pp. 194–5.

22. *OC* iv, p. 199.

23. Ibid., p. 208.

24. Ibid., p. 215.

25. Ibid., v, pp. 20–1.

26. Ibid., v, p. 44.

27. Ibid., v, p. 84. Note that Debauve gives a useful description of Léon Vanier in *Laforgue en son Temps*, pp. 23–9.

28. *LA*, p. 45.

29. Debauve obtained both the proof sheets for *Les Complaintes* and Laforgue's letters to Léon Vanier from his, Debauve's, uncle, Charles Martyne who bought them from Vanier himself on or about 25 April 1899. M. Debauve naturally gives an account of this in *Laforgue en son Temps*.

30. Debauve, p. 79.

31. See *OC* v, pp. 84–5.
32. Ibid., pp. 92–3.
33. Debauve, p. 85.
34. *LA*, p. 71. It would be wrong not to note that caution is needed over this chronology, because of G. Jean-Aubry's speculation over dates. Some of the dates he gives are obviously wrong. Others may be.
35. *LA*, p. 74.
36. Ibid., p. 79.
37. Ibid., p. 86.
38. *OC* v, p. 120.
39. Debauve, p. 95. See also *OC* v, p. 126.
40. Ibid., pp. 182–4.
41. Story has it that the manuscripts disappeared from the Jacques Doucet library in Paris during the German occupation.

SELECT BIBLIOGRAPHY

I. LAFORGUE'S WORKS

1. *Verse*

Les Complaintes, Paris (Vanier), 1885.
L'Imitation de Notre-Dame la Lune, Paris (Vanier), 1886.
Le Concile féerique, Paris (Publications de la Vogue), 1886.
Les Derniers Vers de Jules Laforgue, Tours (Deslis), 1890.
Poésies Complètes, Paris (Vanier), 1894.

2. *Prose*

Moralités légendaires, Paris (Librairie de la Revue Indépendante), 1887.
Lettres à un ami. 1880-86, Paris (Mercure de France), 1941.
Stéphane Vassiliew, Geneva (P. Cailler), 1946.

3. *Collected Works*

Œuvres complètes de Jules Laforgue, 4 volumes, Paris (Mercure de France), 1902-3: Vol. i, *Moralités légendaires;* Vol. ii and Vol. iii, *Poésies* Vol. iv, *Mélanges posthumes.*

Editions de la Connaissance, 3 volumes, Paris 1920-1: Vol. i, *Chroniques parisiennes;* Vol. ii, *Dragées. Charles Baudelaire. Tristan Corbière;* Vol. iii, *Exil. Poésies. Spleen.*

Select Bibliography

Œuvres complètes de Jules Laforgue, 6 volumes, Paris (Mercure de France), 1922-30: Vols. i and ii, *Poésies;* Vol. iii, *Moralités légendaires:* Vols. iv and v, *Lettres;* Vol. vi, *En Allemagne. Berlin, la cour et la ville. Une vengeance à Berlin.* This volume also includes the *Agenda* for 1883.

4. Miscellaneous

Walt Whitman. *Œuvres choisies* [Poèmes en prose traduite par Jules Laforgue...], Paris (Editions N.R.F.), 1918.

5. Recent Editions

Complaintes. L'Imitation de Notre-Dame la Lune. Derniers Vers (ed. Claude Pichois), Paris, 1959.
Derniers Vers (eds. Collie and L'Heureux), Toronto, 1965.
Poésies complètes (ed. Pascal Pia), Paris, 1970.
Poems (ed. J. A. Hiddlestone), Blackwell, Oxford, 1975.

II. CRITICISM

R. R. Bolgar, 'The Present State of Laforgue Studies', *French Studies* iv (July 1950).
M. Collie, *Laforgue*, Writers and Critics series, Oliver and Boyd, Edinburgh and London, 1963.
J.-L. Debauve, *Laforgue en son Temps*, Editions de la Baconnière, Neuchatel, 1972.
—, *Les Pages de 'la Guepe'*, Nizet, Paris, 1970.
R. de Souza, 'Un Cinquantenaire: Jules Laforgue', *Mercure de France*, ccxxix, 1937.
M. Dufour, *Etude sur l'Esthétique de Jules Laforgue*, Vanier, Paris, 1904.
E. Dujardin, 'Les Premiers Poètes du Vers Libre', *Mercure de France*, cxlvi, 1921.
M.-J. Durry, *Jules Laforgue*, Seghers, Paris, 1952.
C. Ephrussi, 'Exposition des Artistes indépendants', *Gazette des Beaux-Arts*, i, 1880, pp, 485-8.
E. J. H. Greene, 'Jules Laforgue et T. S. Eliot', *Revue de littérature comparée*, 22nd year (July-September 1948), pp. 363-97.
—, *T. S. Eliot et la France*, Boivin, Paris, 1951.
F. C. Golffing, 'Jules Laforgue', *Quarterly Review of Literature*, No. 1, Summer 1946, pp. 56-67.
D. Grojnowski, 'La Poétique de Laforgue', *Critique*, No. 237, February 1967.
L. Guichard, *Jules Laforgue et ses poésies*. Presses universitaires de France, Paris, 1950.

J. K. Huysmans, 'Le Salon de 1879', in *Œuvres Complètes*, Vol. vi, Editions G. Crès et Cie, Paris, 1929, pp, 101-43.

G. Kahn, *Symbolistes et décadents*, Vanier, Paris, 1902.

—, 'Jules Laforgue', *Les Hommes d'Aujourd'hui*, vi, No. 298.

C. Mauclair, *Essai sur Jules Laforgue*, Mercure de France, Paris, 1896.

F. de Miomandre, 'Jules Laforgue', *Mercure de France*, xlv, 1903.

E. Pound, 'Irony, Laforgue and some Satire', *Poetry*, xi, No.2, November 1917, reprinted in *Literary Essays of Ezra Pound*, Faber, London, 1960.

—, 'A Study of French Poets', reprinted in *Make it New*, Faber, London, 1925, pp. 159-247.

W. Ramsey, *Laforgue and the Ironic Inheritance*, Oxford University Press, New York, 1953.

—, (ed.), *Essays on a Poet's Life and Work*, Southern Illinois University Press, 1969.

P. Reboul, *Laforgue*, Collection 'Connaissance des Lettres', Paris, 1960.

F. Ruchon, *Laforgue, sa vie, son œuvre*, Albert Ciana, Geneva, 1924.

A. Symons, 'The Decadent Movement in Literature', *Harpers' New Monthly Magazine*, lxxxvii, November 1894, pp. 858-67.

—, *The Symbolist Movement in Literature*, Heinmann, London, 1899.

René Taupin, *L'Influence du Symbolisme français sur la Poésie américaine*, Librairie Honoré Champion, 1929.

M. Turnell, 'Jules Laforgue', *Scrutiny*, v, No. 2, 1939.

—, 'Jules Laforgue', *Cornhill Magazine*, London, No. 973, Winter 1947-8, pp. 74-90.

L. Venturi, *Les Archives de l'Impressionnisme: Lettres de Renoir, Monet, Pissarro, Sisley et Autres. Mémoires de Paul Durand-Ruel. Documents*, Burt Franklin, New York, 1968, Vols. i and ii, pp. 7-112.

I. de Wyzewa, 'Carnet de 1884-5', *Mercure de France*, October–November 1953.

E. Zola, *Mon Salon. Manet. Ecrits sur l'Art*, ed. Antoinette Ehrard, Garnier-Flammarion, Paris, 1970.